Bungalow Style

Bungalow Style

CREATING CLASSIC INTERIORS
IN YOUR
ARTS AND CRAFTS HOME

TREENA CROCHET

The Taunton Press

The Taunton Press, Inc., 63 South Main Street, PO Box 5506, Newtown, CT 06470-5506
e-mail: tp@taunton.com

Editor: Erica Sanders-Foege
Front jacket design: Lori Wendin
Back jacket/spine design: Sandra Mahlstedt
Interior design and layout: Susan Fazekas
Illustrator: Melanie Powell
Photographer: Randy O'Rourke
Front cover photographer: Roe A. Osborn, © The Taunton Press, Inc.

Library of Congress Cataloging-in-Publication Data

Crochet, Treena.
  Bungalow style : creating classic interiors in your arts and crafts home / Treena Crochet.
    p. cm.
  ISBN 1-56158-623-4
  1. Bungalows--Conservation and restoration--United States. 2. Dwellings--
Remodeling-- United States. 3. Arts and crafts movement--Influence.
  4. Interior decoration--United States--History--21st century. I. Title.
  NA7571.C765 2005
  747'.88373--dc22
                              2004009748

Printed in Singapore
10 9 8 7 6 5 4 3

*For my parents,
Robert and
Elizabeth Vleck*

Acknowledgments

THERE ARE MANY PEOPLE who offered their advice, criticism, expertise, and support throughout the research and writing of this book. I am indebted to all at The Taunton Press who worked together to make this project a reality: Helen Albert, executive editor, offered the vision; Randy O'Rourke offered his critical eye as the photographer; developmental editor Erica Sanders-Foege put her voice with mine to edit the text; and photo editor Wendi Mijal and design manager Rosalind Wanke used their creative talents to put it all together. Also, thanks to Jenny Peters for all her help in keeping the project on track.

A special thanks to all the homeowners who allowed Randy and me to take over their homes for the grueling two-day photo shoots.

Finally, I wish to acknowledge Virginia Commonwealth University School of the Arts in Qatar, which supported the writing of this book through a research grant.

Contents

Why Re-Create Classic Interiors?

There's something special about living in a home that's more than simply old. In fact, few experiences are as gratifying as owning a piece of history and returning it to its former beauty. Even if you never literally strap on the tool belt, actively participating in the various stages of planning, research, and rebuilding allows you to feel much more connected to your home.

On a practical level, bringing harmony to your home's historical style simply looks better. Done right, it's a tremendous boost in your real-estate investment, increasing not only the value of your home but also likely improving your neighborhood, too. In the end, seeing the final result of your hard work and determination is the greatest reward.

Houses in the Arts and Crafts and Bungalow styles, whether historic or newly built, transport us back to a simpler time. Life today is hectic and complicated—it only makes sense that we yearn for the good old days. Arts and Crafts– and Bungalow-style houses, which date from the late 1800s to around 1930, are precious symbols of America's growth and prosperity.

Renovating these romantic gems—or building one new—presents its own set of challenges, both physical and mental. The layout and amenities of Arts and Crafts and Bungalow homes are often outdated for the American family in the twenty-first century. For example, most Bungalows have just one bathroom, which is not enough for the way we live. And many of us are more comfortable with an eat-in kitchen, preferably combined with a family room. In a classic Bungalow- or Arts and Crafts–style home, this layout doesn't exist.

On the mental side of the equation, many homeowners are daunted by the idea of taking on such a monumental project. As an interior designer, I get asked all the time, "How can I restore my house to its pristine roots without giving up modern conveniences?" The answer is not an easy one. Whole books, magazines, and cable-network shows are dedicated to the topic.

But as I tell my clients, no matter what the situation, there is always a solution. The most important step is uncovering the home's original bones. Then begins the planning process, where it's important to take into consideration the scope of work, budgetary constraints, time commitment, and finding the right specialists to

carry out the work. Of course, new homes built in these styles present their own challenges.

This book is meant to be used as a guide. Here, you'll find the ideas and tools to make smart decisions about undertaking such a project with sensitivity to your home's historic character. In the following chapters, you'll find plenty of inspiring restorations, renovations, and new homes that run the gamut from the near-museum-quality authentic to the more mainstream to the very grand. I'll begin by identifying and illustrating the major architectural hallmarks of the Arts and Crafts and Bungalow styles. Next, I'll discuss exterior and interior features most characteristic of the period, from rooflines and window placement to decorative details. Chapter 2 offers an in-depth look at woodwork typical of the Arts and Crafts period. In chapter 3, I'll cover more interior details, focusing on wall treatments and color schemes and also how to treat ceilings and floors.

The final chapters examine updating these precious gems of history for modern living. "Finding and Creating Space" (chapter 4) looks at how to creatively expand or redesign your Arts and Crafts– or Bungalow-style home, for example, by reconfiguring a bathroom space or adding on to a modern kitchen. The last chapter examines how to create a classic interior, integrating modern amenities such as heating and cooling systems and lighting. Throughout the book, you'll find inspiring case studies that offer real-life solutions to updating and renovating questions.

Whether you are renovating or building a new home in an old style, it's my hope that this book will enlighten you about how to enjoy your vintage—or vintage-style—home while living in the twenty-first century.

ONE

What Style Is Your Home?

ROM THE 1700S COLONIAL to the 1950s Ranch, few house styles have caught the eye of American homeowners more than the Arts and Crafts and Bungalow styles. Beloved in their own time, these houses are enjoying a much-deserved renaissance.

These popular architectural styles find their roots in the Arts and Crafts movement. From this rich design aesthetic, the Bungalow came to be, representing a more modest version of the Arts and Crafts home. Originally built in planned neighborhoods throughout America during the early 1900s, these small but quaint homes—Bungalows—represented some of the most forward-thinking American architecture.

Innovative in their designs, Bungalows were not only comfortable but also practical. They incorporated beautiful details as well as economical built-ins such as chests, bookcases, and window seats. Well-equipped kitchens and baths were standard features in both Arts and Crafts and Bungalow homes.

It goes without saying that Bungalow design owes much to the Arts and Crafts movement itself. One of the most important components of the movement's style, popularized by architect and designer William Morris during the late 1800s, was the value placed on using natural materials inside and out. For example, exteriors featured simple post-and-beam construction with wood shingle- or stone-clad walls. Well-crafted interiors incorporated rustic elements such as wood, tile, art glass, and metalwork.

◄ Hugging the low Midwestern plains, this 1917 Prairie-style home shows Frank Lloyd Wright's influence with its prominent hip roof, leaded glass windows, and horizontal bands of contrasting materials.

Taking cues from the Arts and Crafts movement, American architects began designing homes in harmony with nature. Before the Arts and Crafts style evolved, there were Shingle homes, which blended organic materials and a balance of proportion and scale, tempered by premier craftsmanship. In the late 1800s, Shingle homes stood in stark contrast to the heavily ornate Queen Anne Victorians that were so prevalent. The Shingle style was perhaps one of the last important contributions of Victorian architecture and its influence can be seen in the Arts and Crafts– and Bungalow-style home.

CRAFTSMAN, PRAIRIE, OR MISSION STYLE?

Many don't realize it, but as Arts and Crafts homes led to Bungalows, so, too, did Bungalows across the country evolve into three distinct housing types. When you hear the terms "Craftsman," "Prairie," and "Mission" style, often the image of a generic Arts

▼ Built in 1908 by Greene and Greene, the Gamble House in Pasadena, Calif., epitomizes the Arts and Crafts style. Flattened gables and sweeping horizontal lines contribute to the house's low profile. Deeply shaded eaves with exposed rafter ends and moss-green shingles contrast with brick chimneys.

and Crafts house comes to mind. Likely, you'll think of the popular Gamble House by Southern California architects Charles and Henry Greene. Or if you're from the Midwest, you may think of a Frank Lloyd Wright Prairie-style home. Texans may see a home with arched doorways and a tiled roof, hallmarks of the local Mission style.

Each of these terms describes a specific style that evolved from the Arts and Crafts movement in America. Driven by the basic tenets of the movement, each is heavily focused on incorporating natural materials.

Mainly, these style differences are regional. The Prairie style finds its roots in the Midwest, the Mission in the Southwest, and the Craftsman spread across the country. People helped shape these styles, too. A vocal proponent of the Arts and Crafts movement, Gustav Stickley created the Craftsman home. Prairie refers to the work of Wright and his Prairie School of architects. Mission evolved from the Spanish architecture of the mission churches that proliferated from Mexico.

EMERGING STYLES

Placing houses into neat categories is nearly impossible. One type does not die out before the next appears. History has shown that emerging styles incorporate much from previous architectural periods, continually developing as time and culture shape the style's direction.

This is true for the Arts and Crafts and Bungalow styles, which emerged partly in reaction to the heavily ornamented Victorian home. Later, during the 1920s, the classic Bungalow would find itself overshadowed by the Neo-Colonial style that was coming into vogue. Many Bungalows built in the late 1920s, for example, featured painted woodwork. Bathrooms took on a new formality with white porcelain and pristine tile. By the 1930s, the popularity of Bungalows had passed.

Fortunately, Americans today have rediscovered the appeal of Arts and Crafts and Bungalow homes. By restoring whole houses—inside and out—homeowners are experiencing just how adaptable and beautiful these now-vintage homes can be. And through renovations that remain sensitive to the original structures, homeowners are preserving a little of our architectural heritage.

▲ The launch of Gustav Stickley's magazine *The Craftsman* in 1901 made the modest Bungalow the most popular American house from 1905 to 1930.

▲ Typical of the Arts and Craft style, this mica-shaded lantern from 1909 recalls mythical fashions popular in English cottages.

Craftsman Style

Perhaps the most widely copied style to come out of the Arts and Crafts movement—and the houses it spawned—was the modest Craftsman Bungalow. Like the Shingle style, the Craftsman home relied on organic materials to anchor itself to its site and to the environment. The Prairie and Craftsman styles shared many similarities. They both featured organic materials: wood for siding and millwork; clay for bricks and tile; and copper, iron, and bronze forged into decorative hardware for windows and doors. Stickley defined Craftsman design in America. Like the English architect William Morris, Stickley was a firm believer that homes and their furnishings should reflect quality craftsmanship. His magazine, *The Craftsman*, which made its debut in 1901, introduced the public to his vision for a housing style based on exteriors and interiors that were created nearly as one unit. Designs featured in the magazine included uncomplicated interiors with clean lines, plaster walls, and exposed beams.

The Craftsman offered scaled house plans that served as the background for his furniture designs. Stickley's imitators were many.

Bungalow- or Craftsman-style homes, which prevailed from about 1890 through the 1920s, were often small in scale—one to one-and-a-half stories in size—and had gabled roofs. Like Shingle-style architecture, these houses were designed to blend into the surrounding environment. They featured deep-shaded porches with plain rails or heavy posts. Windows and doors often contained brightly colored art glass or beveled glass, which also could be found throughout the interior in the glass fronts of built-in cabinetry.

▼ A 1914 Bungalow in California reflects Craftsman styling with its projecting attic story, welcoming porch, and exposed rafter gables.

Hallmarks of the Craftsman Style (1890–1920)

- Small house sizes fitting into planned neighborhoods
- Typically one to one-and-a-half stories in size with a low, gabled roof
- Like the Shingle style, designed to blend into the surrounding environment
- "Deep-shaded" porches on the front side with plain rail or heavy post designs
- Art glass and beveled glass in select windows and doors

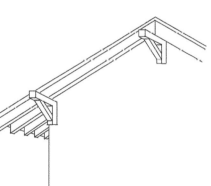

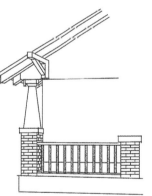

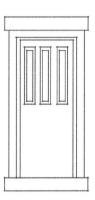

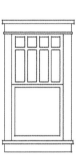

Low gabled roof with projecting rafters

Deep shaded porches

Divided glazing in the upper sash

Grid design in the upper sash

Prairie Style

Wright's Prairie School created what is known today as the Prairie-style home. Not surprisingly, the Midwest has some of the best examples of distinctive Prairie homes, since this is where Wright did most of his work in the early 1900s.

These simple, unobtrusive structures hugged the earth as they spread horizontally across the site. Alternating bands of materials such as brick and concrete created horizontal lines that directed the eyes laterally across the front of the house. Hipped roofs established the low profile. Important hallmarks of the Prairie style include a hipped roof over the second-story bedrooms and porch areas designed with deep eaves—essential for shading the inside in a time before air-conditioning.

While the exaggerated overhanging eaves blocked direct sunlight, they also created deep shadows along the home's facade, adding to its dramatic look. Colorful art glass in windows and doors also played an important part in the Prairie style, bringing decorative patterns of light and color to the home's interior.

▲ This Prairie-style addition mimics features from the original house. The heavily proportioned brick pillar posts were copied from the front porch. Beveled glass dresses up the doors, while geometric designs of colored art glass filter light through transoms above.

▼ The dormer window in this one-story Texas Bungalow brings fresh air into the attic and feeds a large fan that distributes cool air throughout the house.

◄ This modest Bungalow maintains elements of the Prairie style with its low-hipped roof and deep, overhanging eaves. Establishing a visual balance between roof and structure, thin bands of concrete define the porch and terrace area.

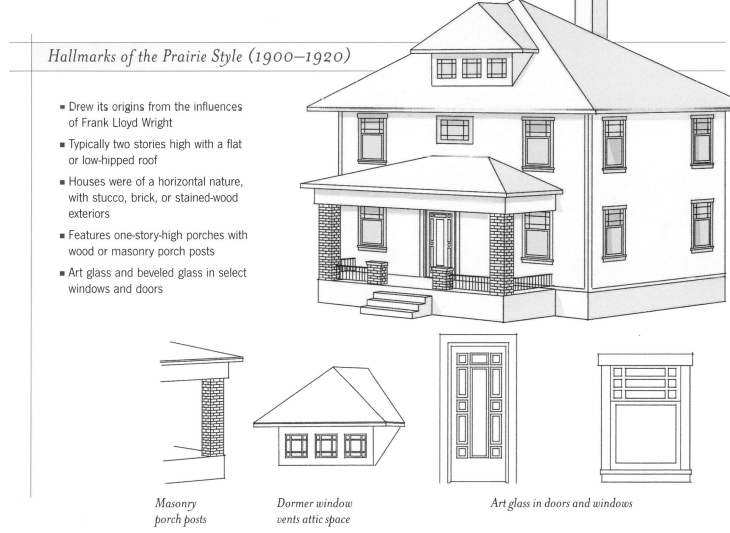

Hallmarks of the Prairie Style (1900–1920)

- Drew its origins from the influences of Frank Lloyd Wright

- Typically two stories high with a flat or low-hipped roof

- Houses were of a horizontal nature, with stucco, brick, or stained-wood exteriors

- Features one-story-high porches with wood or masonry porch posts

- Art glass and beveled glass in select windows and doors

Masonry porch posts

Dormer window vents attic space

Art glass in doors and windows

Mission Style

The Mission Bungalow gets its name from the Spanish missions that inspired them. During the 1700s, Spanish missions began to appear in parts of California, Texas, and Florida. The style is characterized by the use of stucco, brick, or ashlar masonry, which used rough-cut stones, in a building's construction. Clay was used to form barrel-tile roofing and Moorish-inspired tile designs. Like most derivative styles of the Arts and Crafts movement, Mission style evolved during the late 19th century and fell out of fashion by the late 1920s as a new Spanish Colonial style emerged.

The style also often featured modestly sized structures, typically one story with a small attic space. Round arches were common, recalling the mission cloister with stucco or rough, plastered interior walls. Just as in old missions, some homes had elaborate decorative features including vivid art glass.

▶ The arch is a key element of Mission Bungalows. Here, the rhythm of the facade is established through the arched window and door openings. The red-clay tile roof, a typical feature, accentuates the peaks of the attic space in this Dallas, Tex., 1930 Bungalow.

The Shingle Style (1880–1900)

The Shingle style was a precursor to the emerging Arts and Crafts aesthetic. Like most Victorian homes of the late 19th century, Shingle houses were large scale, often two or even three stories tall, and featured eyebrow dormers on multiple-gabled roofs. Unlike the stately Victorian, the Shingle home made rich use of simple, organic materials in design and construction.

Clad in naturally stained wood-shake siding, these impressive houses included expansive, deep porches, which made for clear outdoor views. Like Bungalows, the porch posts and balustrades were also finished in shingles or made from stone to blend in with the surrounding landscape.

Shingle-style interiors reflected the natural environment by incorporating stained—not painted—wood moldings, wainscoting, and flooring. Predating William Morris's prints, walls were covered in botanical-patterned papers. Organically inspired clay tiles graced fireplaces.

Here both shingles and wood trim are stained dark brown so that the house blends in with the tall trees that surround it.

Hallmarks of the California Mission Style (1890–1920)

- More prevalent in states with a Spanish past, particularly California, Texas, and Florida
- Small house size, typically one story
- Barrel-tile roofs
- Moorish towers or Spanish-influenced details
- Round arches recalling a mission cloister
- Plain but functional interiors
- Some art glass

Arched doors   Casement windows   Arched windows   Barrel-tile roof

Architectural Hallmarks

Owners of period-style homes appreciate the fine distinction that makes these homes so desirable to live in. Regardless of the style of your Arts and Crafts or Bungalow home, whether Prairie, Craftsman, or Mission, knowing when it was built and learning about architectural hallmarks will help you understand its unique characteristics and charm. For many people, this process of discovery is one of the most exciting things about restoring or renovating a vintage home.

Exterior and interior elements are treated similarly among the various styles. Features such as hipped or gabled rooflines, art-glass windows, and deep-shaded porches, coupled with interior features such as highly figured woodwork, handcrafted tile fireplaces, and glazed door designs are common to most Arts and Crafts and Bungalow homes.

Local builders and craftsmen constructed these homes, though, so not only do the houses reflect individual style differences but also regional ones. A Bungalow in Chicago, for example, contains little of the Spanish influence that you're likely to discover in one in, say, Dallas.

MODEST SCALE

Unlike the large-scale Victorian homes of the late 19th century—or even the early Arts and Crafts homes that were constructed during the same period—the size of a Bungalow was smaller and more compact in its planning and design. Families moved into planned neighborhoods on the outskirts of cities that consisted of more modest one- to one-and-a-half-story Bungalows.

Careful planning on the designer's part took advantage of space on the ground floor. There were adequate living and dining rooms, a kitchen, a bathroom, a sleeping porch, and two small bedrooms. Two-story Bungalows featured the bedrooms on the second story, and even more upscale models offered an additional bathroom.

▶ **This typical Craftsman Bungalow features multiple gables not only covering the house but also the porch and attic vent. Rafter ends protruding from the recessed eaves are common to smaller-scaled Bungalows.**

▼ **This Bungalow from 1911 is classic Craftsman in its design and use of materials. The shingle-clad siding provides textural contrast to the river-rock foundation below, while the sloping gable roof is highlighted by exposed end rafters.**

What follows is a sampling of each style, highlighting common features as well as regional differences. These examples will help you identify the style most closely resembling your own home, whether it's a Prairie, Craftsman, or Mission Bungalow or in the Arts and Crafts style.

ROOFLINES

In the simple Arts and Crafts and Bungalow styles, the roof set the tone for the house. One-story Craftsman-style Bungalows featured a gently sloping gabled roof with a low, wide dormer on the front that vented the attic. Often, the gables crossed in a variety of configurations, mostly following the arrangement of the space beneath. Front porches often had their own roofs, which were reduced in size and profile to fit the scale of the enclosing space.

▲ The chimney dominates the facade of this classic Southern California Bungalow built in 1912. Porch piers establish the taper theme, creating a striking massive effect. The stone and brick pattern, called "peanut brittle," is common to the area.

▲ Oak doors with colorful, geometric art-glass panes relieve the heavy texture of shingle siding and rough-cut stone used on retaining walls and walkways of this California Bungalow from 1912.

Two-story Craftsman-style Bungalows had the same sloping gabled roof, but the steeper pitch from ridgeline to the first floor provided a more dramatic sweep. Second-story bedrooms were ventilated through a cross-gabled configuration or expanded dormer windows, which also provided more light.

Prairie-style roofs utilized a low, hugging hip roof similar to the ones seen on Wright's designs. In fact, in warmer climates where snow was not a concern, such as Southern California and Florida, the roofs of Prairie Bungalows appeared almost flat.

WINDOWS

One of the most consistent features of Prairie, Mission, and Craftsman Bungalows is the division of door and window glass into grid-like arrangements of the muntins. Where there are both sash and casement windows, the consistent muntin pattern establishes a set rhythm throughout the house.

Window designs typically incorporated divided-light panels in the upper sash, leaving one large pane of glass in the lower sash. The

▶ Strong linear patterns emphasize the vertical design of the front entry of this Prairie style home, establishing balance between the front door and side panels.

larger panes became more widely available as glass-making techniques improved. This open panel in the lower sash brought in views of the outdoors, which was key to reinforcing the idea of setting the Bungalow within its natural environment.

A recurring element in these styles was the incorporation of both art glass and beveled glass. Although designs may vary from purely geometric to botanical or foliate patterns, art glass added character to an otherwise ordinary window and provided filtered privacy as well. Often, art-glass windows appeared in living rooms, flanking the fireplace, or in areas such as entry stairwells, where the highly decorative glass became the focal point of the space.

Beveled glass, clearly defined by lead muntins, was seen in grander Bungalows and was a dominant feature of Prairie-style houses. The beveling of leaded glass refracts the light, adding sparkle and dimension to an otherwise flat surface.

▲ This 1931 Mission-style Bungalow in California features strong Moorish characteristics. The arched entry door mimics the pointed arch window of the living room. A stone path leads visitors directly to the front door and balances the visual weight of the barrel-tile roof.

ENTRYWAYS

With Arts and Crafts and Bungalow homes, front doors were designed in conjunction with the window style, whether rectangular for Prairie and Craftsman styles or arched for Mission. Regardless of shape, the front entry framed the house and gave a welcoming feel. The entry complemented the window pattern by integrating beveled-glass or art-glass panes in its design. While the placement of entry doors varied from direct center to off-center, in most cases the doors were protected by the deep shadows of the front porch.

Whether the door was constructed of stately oak or painted wood, the hardware was often of hammered copper, forged iron, or cast bronze—a direct influence of the Arts and Crafts movement, which emphasized that a craftsman's work be evident in the finished product.

▲ This small Prairie Bungalow is all roof and columns, with its exaggerated overhang and strong front-porch pillars. Oversized planters frame the steps leading up to the outdoor space, a typical Prairie touch.

PORCHES

Porches were an integral part of the design. Essential in blending the house with its natural surroundings, porches were an extension of the living space. A holdover from the grand Victorians and Shingle style, the generous size of Bungalow front porches was a quaint reminder of a more leisurely lifestyle when evenings were spent watching the passersby and taking in cool nighttime breezes.

Whether placed directly in the middle or off to the side, the front porch was typically reached by taking a paved walkway. Framed by pillar posts and often protected by a front-facing gabled roof, the porch made a welcoming first impression to all who entered the home.

▲ A closer look at the porte cochere in this 1907 home reveals masonry work combining brick and river rock that was common to Southern California Bungalows.

▲ No Bungalow is complete without its outdoor porch. This one gives the homeowners full view of the neighborhood with its open railing construction.

Materials used in its construction were meant to complement the overall design of the main house, whether shingle clad, rubble stone, or stucco.

Just as important but perhaps not as visible was the enclosed sleeping porch common to most Bungalows. Three walls of screened casement or sash windows brought in night breezes to cool the room. Sleeping porches typically appeared on the rear of the house, yet some second-story examples were located on the front of the house. In many renovation projects, the sleeping porch provided adequate space for expansion when adding an additional bathroom, kitchen, or family room.

▲ This 1911 Craftsman-style home features an enclosed sleeping porch with casement windows on three walls. The windows open wide to bring in the cool night breezes.

Architectural Influences

In the late 1800s, a new generation of primarily English architects rejected Victorian design and all it represented. In the new industrial age, machine-wrought style was thought to be heavy and impersonal. Architects and designers of the Arts and Crafts movement began experimenting with fresh attitudes toward modern living and design.

In the United States, Frank Lloyd Wright, Gustav Stickley, and Charles and Henry Greene were among those architectural innovators. With a renewed focus on form, simple construction, and craftsmanship, they built homes in a new American style. Their visions caught the attention of many like-minded designers and homeowners. Soon their imitators were many.

GUSTAV STICKLEY

Stickley was a successful American entrepreneur who was instrumental in bringing the Arts and Crafts movement to the United States from England. Heavily influenced by the writings of William Morris, the movement's leader, Stickley designed interiors that reflected Arts and Crafts ideals. In 1901, he launched *The Craftsman* magazine. Soon it was published widely, and Americans became well acquainted with the charming Bungalow style.

FRANK LLOYD WRIGHT

Although the Prairie style is most associated with Wright, there were many architects who worked in a similar direction at the time. The Prairie style that Wright created was adapted and developed by architects designing early Bungalow housing kits.

SPANISH MISSIONS

Since the Colonial era, Catholic missionaries from Mexico had settled throughout Texas, California, and the Southwest. Their mission churches reflected the Moorish architecture of their native Spain with arched doorways, tiled roofs, and ornate bell towers. As these stone edifices endured, their design became a part of the local architectural heritage.

Interior Details

The Bungalow represented one of the most efficiently designed housing types, incorporating many space-saving devices such as built-in chests, bookcases, and window seats. For the first time in American architecture, interior space planning opened the dining room to the living room, only hinting at separation through an abbreviated room divider.

In addition to being affordable, these well-designed houses brought the latest technologies into the home, such as indoor plumbing and electricity, and made use of quality materials inside and out.

Bungalow interiors reveal overlapping Craftsman, Prairie, and Mission influences. Characteristics such as rich hardwood millwork, organic finish materials such as clay tiles for fireplace surrounds and flooring, and mineral-rich hardware are hallmarks of the interior style.

KIT HOMES

Mail-order catalog companies such as Sears, Roebuck and Co. and Aladdin offered a well-equipped kit of plans, building specifications, and materials—all shipped by railcar to the desired location. These kit homes capitalized on the public's interest in Arts and Crafts–influenced styles. The manufacturers offered floor plans ranging in size from two to four bedrooms and of various design combinations.

WOODWORK

In determining the origins of a home, it's important to look at the woodwork used throughout the interior. Entry foyers often featured superbly crafted inglenooks. Wainscoted walls with wide caps encircled whole rooms. Boxed ceiling beams outlined and divided the ceiling plane. Many details such as crown moldings, door and window trim, stairwells, room dividers, flooring, and

▼ A Prairie-style Bungalow uses a series of beveled-glass pocket doors to separate the living room, dining room, and den. Pocket doors, a holdover from the Victorian era, open up space in the modest Bungalow layout.

The Open Layout

The efficiency of the Bungalow design relies on open and connected spaces. Here, a half-wall room divider designates separate living and dining spaces and maintains a visual connection between rooms.

Three-over-one windows flank the fireplace.

Tapered pillar posts emphasize mass.

Window casing matches millwork details.

Built-ins display geometrically arranged muntin glass fronts.

The cased opening is heavy.

The lower sash features large-sized glass panels.

An Emphasis on Craftsmanship

A foyer in this newly built Shingle-style home borrows from the style of English Arts and Crafts designer Charles Voysey. Wooden beams divide and compress the ceiling, while quartersawn white oak defines door and window openings. In the entryway, wainscoting visually ties in with the stair railing.

Quartersawn white oak defines the door and window openings.

Exposed beams divide the ceiling.

Charles Voysey-inspired millwork decorates the newel and posts.

Wainscoting ties the entry space to the stair landing.

built-ins were a direct reflection of the Arts and Crafts movement in America and Stickley's Craftsman influence.

Although the types of wood varied with the styling of the house, from high-end Arts and Crafts– and Prairie-style Bungalows to smaller-scaled Craftsman homes, fine woodwork featured rich grain patterns of oak, red pine, gumwood, or fir. These grains were further emphasized with the application of darkening stains over natural finishes. Particularly in the South and Southwest, Bungalow homes built during the 1920s featured painted woodwork details as part of the original scheme. This was an attempt to modernize the look and capitalize on an emerging Neo-Colonial style.

Bungalow interiors relied on organic materials to complete the architectural scheme. Combined textures of natural materials used throughout the interior created visual interest, as seen in window seats, inglenooks, built-in cabinets, and bookcases combining wood, glass, and metals in their design and construction.

▲ In smaller, two-story Bunga-lows, staircases are often tucked in a hallway off the main entry. In this Prairie house, the stair is considered a key architectural element, alluding to the grand nature of the style.

WALLS, CEILINGS, AND FLOORS

A careful selection and application of finishes and materials subtly brought together the Arts and Crafts and Bungalow home's open floor plan. Wallpapers, stenciling, or painted plaster, in conjunction with a palette of highly saturated terra cottas, delicate sage greens, and golden yellows, worked to establish flow from room to room. The Arts and Crafts celebration of flora and fauna was reiterated in themes featured in wallpaper, tile, and carpeting.

▲ This Arts and Crafts interior incorporates natural patterns and textures in its design, as seen in the rich wood grain of the oak, the clay tile floor, and William Morris reproduction wallpaper. Photo © www.carolynbates.com, Sandra Vitzthum Architect, LLC.

Quiet Spaces

A space-saving feature, this inglenook located at one end of the dining room offers a quiet reading space after meals and is conveniently close to the kitchen. Coordinating wallpapers and paint colors connect the space to the rest of the interior.

Foliate designs adorn the wall.

Built-in bookcases flank the window.

Wall sconces offer soft lighting.

Geometric paneling adds visual interest.

Inglenook bench provides seating and storage.

▲ This original kitchen in a Sears Bungalow kit home has conveniently apportioned storage with cabinetry above and below. Generous four-over-one windows add to the sense of openness.

KITCHENS

As the American middle class grew, so did the demand for housing that would accommodate the working lifestyle. In response, Bungalow homes, as descendants of the Arts and Crafts style, were designed with kitchens large enough in which to cook and clean. Homemakers, not domestic servants, would use fully equipped kitchens. Modern conveniences added functionality to the room that was never known before. Electric appliances were built in. And, in many cases, instead of hard-to-maintain wood floors, linoleum was installed.

◀ **This new Bungalow-style bathroom offers modern efficiency accented by Craftsman detailing, as seen in the oak vanity, glazed-brick wall tile, and white hexagonal floor tiles.**

BATHROOMS

Bungalow houses were one of the first types to incorporate an integrated bathroom. A combination tub and shower, pedestal sink, and toilet surrounded by ceramic tile promoted hygiene. While these earlier examples featured white tile with small black tile accents, by the late '20s, brightly colored tile and plumbing fixtures were more common.

Cool and Convenient

Often the reality of living in a classic home is less than what you might imagine. If you live in a climate where having air-conditioning is the norm, you'll quickly learn how far from modern your old house is. One solution, besides the window or wall unit, is a high-velocity heating, ventilating, and air-conditioning (HVAC) system. Although expensive, HVAC systems are unobtrusive. And the ductwork often wends around the interior of the walls, so there's little damage done in the installation process. The air conduits are hardly noticeable, placed in out-of-the-way spots such as corners.

HVAC ductwork is hidden in the base of a window seat in this newly constructed Arts and Crafts home. The supply vents blend in with the surrounding woodwork with the help of custom grill covers.

FIREPLACES

The fireplace has long been considered the heart of any house, and in the Arts and Crafts and Bungalow tradition, this did not change. No longer essential to keeping the house well heated, Bungalow fireplaces became a design focal point in the living room.

The fireplace was occasion to display a richness of craftsmanship and contrast. Chunky wooden mantels showed off heavy braces and prominent wood grain. Fireplace surrounds featured handcrafted tile decorated in flora and fauna themes. Natural stone highlighted visual mass and texture.

▼ The mosaic tile surrounding the fireplace in this newly constructed Bungalow adds a touch of color and delicacy to the otherwise rustic mantel and built-in cabinets.

LIGHTING

Bungalows were some of the first homes to be built wired for electricity. It was an exciting time in the lighting industry, and two styles quickly emerged as symbols of the Bungalow aesthetic: the delicate work of Louis Comfort Tiffany and the rustic geometries of Wright. Unfortunately, the fragile lighting did not endure as other interior features did. Today, it's the rare Bungalow that still has its original lighting fixtures.

▲ Where lighting is concerned, many think that only strict geometric designs are appropriate for Bungalow homes. But the delicately shaped lotus-bud glass shades on this original shower fixture are right at home in a 1916 Prairie style residence.

◄ This new Mission features a convenient mudroom with cubbies—another modern amenity.

TWO

Woodwork

WOODWORK IS ESSENTIAL to the style of a house. But as the millwork that had been carefully handcrafted—the doors, windows, mantels, moldings, stairs, and cabinetry—is replaced over time, the home's architectural character becomes obscured. Returning Arts and Crafts and Bungalow homes and their woodwork, or millwork, to their original beauty means doing some research. It means looking to the architectural trends that prevailed at the time.

From about 1900 to the 1930s, American architects and builders produced work that closely followed that of the Arts and Crafts movement in England. Particularly influential were the interiors by William Morris, who designed the entire inside of a house. He was a proponent of using organic materials and emphasized handiwork over anything mass produced. The Arts and Crafts and Bungalow styles evolved, in part, as a reaction against heavy Victorian ornament, so the woodwork was simpler and more streamlined in design.

In the Bungalow style's early stages, woodwork was unpainted. To give the wood (typically quartersawn oak, chestnut, or maple) an aged patina, the wood was often exposed to ammonia fumes or stained in a dark finish. Other woods used in Arts and Crafts and Bungalow interiors included fir, red gum, red pine, and cypress, depending on the region. These woods, like quartersawn oak, were also chosen for their prominent grain patterns.

Whether stained or painted, woodwork on stairs, built-ins, and window seats became the common denominator for American

◀ **This new addition incorporates woodwork details from the original Prairie-style house, particularly in the design of the doors, windows, and room divider.** ▶ **Window casings emulate crown-molding details in this remodeled Craftsman-style kitchen.**

▲ Delicately shaped leaded-glass panes on these casement windows frame the view of the landscape, outlining each segment as if it were a fine painting. Photo © www.carolynbates.com, Sandra Vitzthum Architect, LLC.

▲ Squared newel posts with oversized caps define each turn of this staircase.

▲ A holdover from earlier styles, this simple batten door adorned with wrought-iron scrollwork and hardware provides textural contrast to the shingle siding, underlining the overall rustic look of the Arts and Crafts style. Photo © www.carolynbates.com, Sandra Vitzthum Architect, LLC.

Bungalow homes, which were built for working- and middle-class families during the first 30 years of the 20th century.

Woodwork is such an integral part of the style that determining which is original and which isn't is the key to a successful restoration. Taking clues from existing architectural detailing in areas such as exterior doors and windows, stairs, and built-ins will help you determine whether the other woodwork details in the rest of the house are authentic.

Common woodwork detailing unified doors to windows, moldings to mantels, and stairs to trim and formed cohesion throughout the interior. Echoing the same materials from room to room also set the theme. For example, a front door with a beveled-glass sash and hammered-copper hardware often established a motif for other doors in the house.

MAKING A VISUAL CONNECTION

Stylistic signatures on other woodwork, such as crown moldings and baseboards, give clues as to how doors were framed as well. The lintel over a doorway was often fashioned after the crown-molding profile, although it may have been scaled down to fit the size of the door or cased opening.

Crown-molding designs also impacted the shape and proportions of a fireplace mantel if it was wooden, while window seats, wall paneling, hutches, and closets often incorporated the same profiles, making them appear as a seamless part of the architecture.

◀ The visual connection among doors, window trim, baseboards, and crown moldings are established by repetitive millwork details in this 1912 Arts and Crafts–style home.

▼ This newly constructed Craftsman Bungalow borrows woodwork details from the turn of the 20th century as seen in the implied room divider on the left and the boxed beam spanning the cased opening on the right.

Doors

The entry of any home sets the tone for what's within. In keeping with the Arts and Crafts and Bungalow styles, the doors represented much of what's inherent to the aesthetic. They were typically massive, plain, and clean in their design in order to highlight their natural qualities.

Doors presented the perfect tableau for the highly geometric woodwork detailing that was so much a part of the Arts and Crafts aesthetic. Whether solid panel or partly glazed, many door designs adhered to a strict gridlike pattern influenced by Wright's Prairie style. Others followed Stickley's Craftsman style, based on his interpretations of medieval craft designs. Additional door styles seen in the most basic Bungalows highlighted Arts and

▼ Oversized arched doors command attention in this new Arts and Crafts–style home. Made from tongue-and-groove white oak, the door features hammered-copper hardware and bottle-glass panels. Its design is inspired by the English Arts and Crafts movement with American Shingle-style influences.

▲ A board-and-batten door with elaborate wrought-iron strap hinges reflects the intricacies of ironwork characteristic of Mission-inspired Bungalows. Photo © www.carolynbates.com, Sandra Vitzthum Architect, LLC.

▲ Taking cues from a cabinet door on the original built-in sideboard in the dining room, a replacement door features overscaled strap hinges and a colorful art-glass upper panel.

Crafts simplicity, dividing the door into five evenly spaced recessed panels.

Windowpanes, or glazing, for exterior doors provided a view to the outdoors. Inside, glazing was typically found on double doors that separated a dining space or a private study from the living room. Often, the glass in these doors was compartmentalized into small beveled panes held together with visually prominent lead muntins. Small stained-glass panels frequently appeared in Wright-influenced Prairie-style doors.

Finding Doors

Is your Bungalow missing its original doors? Finding replacements is easier now that many door manufacturers sell them in the Craftsman style. The other option, searching for salvaged doors, might be more of a hunt unless you live in an area where many Bungalows were built, such as Southern California, Minneapolis, and Dallas.

▲ The arched shape of this front door is typical of Mission style-Bungalows and is repeated in the interior on niches, windows, and cased openings.

▶ Double doors dividing the living room from the sunroom feature a faceted glass doorknob. The knobs represent a classic style and, though they are still manufactured today, are hardy enough to survive from renovation to renovation.

▼ This upstairs bedroom door of a Craftsman Bungalow has a basic design: two recessed panels surrounded by slightly fluted trim and a corniced lintel. The door, made from red gumwood, blends nicely with the built-in linen cupboard nearby.

HARDWARE

In the Craftsman style, form and function were closely intertwined where hardware was concerned. This style made use of wrought-iron and hammered-copper hardware, often with over-scaled pieces, which balanced out a door's heavier proportions. In the Prairie doors, brass or bronzed hardware was often fashioned into sleek profiles to underline the lighter design without distracting from rich, glazed panels.

Finer homes from the period featured highly decorative hardware designed in the Arts and Crafts style. Imitating the work of Voysey or Scottish architect Charles Rennie Mackintosh, delicate designs cast out of brass were meant to be buffed and polished to a high sheen.

Another option was glass doorknobs. Glass knobs set against the dark-stained door and cut with small facets captured and reflected light, adding an elegant touch. Sized accordingly, these decorative knobs appeared in other areas of the home, such as on drawers, linen cupboards, and built-ins.

IN HISTORY

Historians regard Arts and Crafts interior design as the forerunner of Modernism with its simple, honest aesthetic. Since the woodwork is plain, the hardware often represents the only ornamentation. At the turn of the 20th century, hardware was sand-cast out of copper, brass, or bronze. This method of casting gave these accessories a handcrafted quality, providing textural relief to the smooth surface of the wood.

▼ A simple brass doorknob adorns the front door of this Prairie home, while an equally plain handle latch is used on the folding doors in the dining room.

▲ Characteristic divided light panels placed in the upper halves of these original Arts and Crafts–style doors separate the formal living room from the recently enclosed porch area.

▲ The most common type of interior door in Bungalow-style homes has five evenly spaced horizontal raised panels inset into simple stiles and rails.

▶ This house features doors with a slight variation of the corner muntin design common to most Prairie-style homes. Instead of one large center sheet of glass, smaller panes divide the panel into multiple rows for safety reasons. The multihinged doors can be collapsed or opened up to an impressive span.

IN HISTORY

Called pebble glass for its rippled appearance, this opaque glazing is made by pressing molten glass into a mold. The resulting texture distorts the glass just enough to allow light to filter through. Glass with this treatment was a popular glazing material for bathroom windows in early Bungalow designs and is still available today.

▲ An elaborate door design dividing the living and dining rooms maintains a formality in this 1916 Prairie-style home. Underlining the grandeur and scale of the house, beveled and leaded glass with art-glass details are framed within mahogany panels. The transom overhead opens to allow for ventilation between spaces.

◄ Beautiful beveled- and leaded-glass doors with diamond-shaped art glass separate the entry foyer from the living room.

The Best of All Styles

THIS PRAIRIE-STYLE HOME, built in 1912, is a lesson learned in trying to neatly define the Arts and Crafts aesthetic. While the external architecture is characteristic of Prairie style, the home's interior styling reflects Arts and Crafts with hints of Neo-Colonial, which gained significant popularity during the 1920s. From the outside, the house features strong Prairie influences with its hipped roof, corniced dormer, and massive square porch supports, yet Moorish finials and a roof made of metal—not shakes nor clay tile—seem out of context.

◄ An original five-panel door, characteristic of the Craftsman style, features an ornately designed brass doorknob with Classical details.

◄ The home's facade remains unchanged since it was built in 1912.

The inside is even more perplexing, as the house contains an amalgam of details. Pocket doors and five-panel doors are accessorized with a combination of Classical and Art Nouveau hardware. Laurel-wreath carvings appear on a newel post and in ceiling medallions, and the painted—not stained—interior woodwork is original.

▼ The large pocket doors are a design feature of Victorian houses that still survive in this Dallas neighborhood. These doors, located between the living and dining rooms, incorporate characteristic Craftsman style into their design by including five recessed panels.

► Another surprising find in the home yet original to its construction, this brass doorknob is fashioned into a fluid Art Nouveau design, which was more popular in Europe from 1895 to 1905 and signified a return to delicate, ornamented design.

Windows

From the diminutive Bungalow to the expansive Arts and Crafts–style home, the most consistent element found in window designs was the use of a single pane of glass on the bottom, or lower, sash. The detailing of the top sash was either decided by the builder or came standard in mail-order kits.

Whether single or double hung, the upper sash was often divided into vertical panels, which varied in number. Windows with three or four divided lights in the upper sash were commonly used in the more modest Bungalows, while upscale homes featured as many as 14—a reflection of finer craftsmanship and detailing. Consistent with Arts and Crafts styling, the divided lights were held in place by thin wood muntins.

Variations on this theme show the top sash divided into smaller diamond shapes, either with wood muntins or strips of lead, which represents a holdover from the Tudor style. It was not uncommon to find both linear and diamond patterns in the upper sash throughout the same house, with the diamond patterns appearing in the more formal rooms such as the living room or library.

Although most windows in Arts and Crafts, Prairie, and Craftsman styles were square or rectangular, Mission-style windows on the street side were often arched as a way to tie in the features of the porch and entryway.

▲ Clerestory windows accommodate the placement of a chest of drawers in the bedroom of this newly constructed Prairie-style home.

▲ Casement windows are often seen in Arts and Crafts and Bungalow homes. Here, glass panes are held in place with lead muntins, complementing the geometry of the wall paneling. Photo © www.carolynbates.com, Sandra Vitzthum Architect, LLC.

◄ Mission-style Bungalows borrowed architectural details from old Spanish mission churches of the Southwest. Here, a large front-facing stained-glass window accentuates the room's cathedral ceiling while incorporating the classic arch motif used in the home's front door, cased openings, and niches.

▲ Raised tripart windows reiterate the arch motif seen in this 1930s Mission-style Bungalow.

IN HISTORY

Simple architectural elements, muntins provide structural support for window glass. These were made from a variety of materials, including stone and lead—as seen in medieval churches—and later, wood. At first, lead muntins were used in windows designed for houses, taking inspiration from the thin lead strips that outlined the details in stained-glass windows. Before sheet glass, windows were made from flattened balloons of molten glass, giving each pane a circular shape. The pliable nature of lead made it easy to follow these small, round shapes of the blown glass. In the 18th century, glass-making techniques improved, resulting in the production of rolled sheet glass. Wood muntins were used to hold these square panes of glass in place, and the small, gridlike patterns they created became synonymous with Colonial-style houses.

▶ The grand scale of this 1916 Arts and Crafts home in Dallas features magnificent stained-glass windows and fine mahogany woodwork.

STAINED GLASS

Another strong characteristic of window design was the incorporation of stained or beveled glass. Stained glass in Arts and Crafts– and Bungalow-style homes was made with metal oxides that gave the glass its color. Leaded glass often had a beveled edge and took its name from the lead, copper, or zinc muntins used to hold it in place. Oxidation, which was not uncommon to these delicate creations, was considered part of the historic character of the glass. The best-maintained windows are those that were cleaned and repaired by glaziers, which was essential to making sure the windows held their value.

◀ The windows in this newly constructed Arts and Crafts–style home were made specifically to showcase the couple's collection of antique stained glass. The windows were custom-made to fit the stained-glass panels with modified sashes on the inside and sheets of protective glass on the outside.

◀ Reiterating the common mix of styles found in Bungalow designs, this stained-glass window features beautifully proportioned classical swags in this 1917 Craftsman home built in a Boston suburb.

John LaFarge

In his day, John LaFarge created works that rivaled those of his contemporary, Louis Comfort Tiffany, although LaFarge is lesser known in the history of American decorative arts. In 1879, he developed the process for making opalescent glass, which he patented. The method involved fusing small pieces of colored glass to create a milky and subtly accented effect. The resulting designs were more elegant and subtle compared with images in other stained glass whose scenes were outlined with leading.

◀ An original LaFarge stained-glass panel, salvaged from a turn-of-the-century home in Boston, illuminates the hallway in this newly constructed Arts and Crafts–style home.

▲ This clerestory window mimics millwork details used on the home's fireplace mantel with its wide-ledge sillplate supported by shaped brackets. The homeowner created her own stained-glass panels hung over the original glass to brighten her simple Sears kit home built in 1910.

▲ The double-hung windows in this Texas-built Sears kit home feature a five-over-one configuration that matches the front door and sidelights. Double-hung windows allow for better airflow with the help of a large attic fan that circulates air throughout the house.

Dard Hunter

Dard Hunter (1883–1966) learned of the Arts and Crafts aesthetic when he stayed at the Riverside Inn in 1903, the first hotel in America built in the style. The following year, he went to work at Roycroft, a community in Pennsylvania for artisans who supported the Arts and Crafts movement. After much persuasion, Hunter became the primary designer of the stained-glass windows for the Roycroft Inn in East Aurora, N.Y. Hunter's trademark design, the Arts and Crafts rose, has been widely copied by others and appears in a variety of stained glass, textile, and pottery pieces.

► The upper sash of this Craftsman style window is divided into 12 uniform panels, which add visual interest and balance to the over-sized lower sash.

◄ A variation of Prairie-style muntin spacing, this window's upper sash is divided into 14 panels, emphasizing a uniform grid pattern at the top. The home, built in 1924, reflects high style with the carefully crafted muntins and brass hardware. As glass became available in larger sizes, homes from the late Victorian era often featured a one-panel lower sash to give unobstructed views to the outdoors.

▲ Accents of stained glass bring color and pattern to the leaded-glass window designs in this dining room.

IN HISTORY

Hinged on their sides, casement windows crank open like a swinging door. Often grouped in pairs, these windows are designed to capture breezes from the outside, provide directional airflow, and ventilate the interior. Casement windows are often seen on the sleeping porches of early Bungalows or in rooms protected by the shade of the outdoor porch.

◄ The bathroom in this 1924 Mission-style home uses pebble or seed glass in the sash areas, which offers privacy.

◄ These casement windows appear in a Sears mail-order Bungalow home located in Texas.

▲ Stained and beveled glass play an important role in Arts and Crafts interiors, as filtered sunlight creates an interesting play of light, color, and shadows.

Trim

Trimwork in Arts and Crafts homes was the most celebrated feature of the interior architecture. It was here in the working of wood for crown moldings, baseboards, door and window trim, and fireplace surrounds and mantels that the Arts and Crafts tradition of quality handiwork was most evident. The simplicity of design, often flat profiles with projecting cornices, broke from the Victorian tradition of elaborate ornamentation.

The trimwork complemented the increasingly popular Mission-style furnishings designed by Gustav Stickley, George Niedecken for Frank Lloyd Wright, and members of the Arts and Crafts community at Roycroft in Pennsylvania, among others. Stickley's magazines showcased his furniture collections in Arts and Crafts homes, which became the basis for the Craftsman style.

As these modest interiors developed, so did the woodwork details that were reiterated from one room to the next. Scale and proportion were carefully considered because the interiors were compact and efficiently designed. Several space-saving features such as built-in inglenooks and window seats, bookcases, hutches, and room dividers were utilized. Ornate or complex moldings would have made the spaces feel too crowded and would have been too overbearing for the architecture, so the design was kept simple.

For as unified and uniform as the designs of these homes were, there was much room for craftsmen to leave their marks. In a variety of homes, the woodwork stood testament to the artisan's individual talent. Whatever the detail, the nuances of style varied from house to house and from region to region. Some homes included understated and restrained Classical details, while others appeared to be inspired by particular designers, such as Charles Mackintosh, who was known for his distinctive grid patterns. These very personal craftsmen's touches were in keeping with the Arts and Crafts movement.

◀ The deep wainscot cap, which offers enough space to use as a display shelf in this newly constructed Craftsman-style home, is historically correct.

▲ Room dividers are designed to maintain a visual flow between spaces while offering separation between the dining and living rooms. The cased opening is capped with a deep cornice that matches the profiles of the window headers. Square, tapering columns lead the eye to glass-fronted built-ins below with Prairie style muntins.

Marketing complete home kits to middle-class consumers via mail-order catalogs, Sears, Roebuck & Co. offered more than 400 styles from Craftsman-inspired Bungalows to Neo-Colonial houses. Each kit included some 30,000 pieces of building materials, each pre-milled and numbered to correlate to a comprehensive instruction manual.

▲ Crown molding in this 1915 Bungalow still has its original picture rail.

▶ This room is a picture of uniformity with its matching door and window trim, set against a plain baseboard with simple quarter-round molding.

▶ Shelving raised high above a beadboard wainscot and supported by tapering brackets is a detail inspired by elements found elsewhere in the existing house for this kitchen remodel.

A Sitting Room with a View

THIS NEWLY BUILT ARTS AND CRAFTS HOME in Massachusetts features a separate sitting room designed with features that offset the angularity of the rest of the house. The shape of the barrel-vaulted ceiling is visually reinforced with a millwork cornice over the recessed sitting area near the windows. Furthering the effect, each stone on the fireplace surround is gently shaped to follow the rhythmic curve of the ceiling, while brackets supporting the mantel shelf are milled with undulating profiles.

Curvilinear lines incorporated into the architecture of this sitting room help relieve the austere geometry found throughout this new Arts and Crafts–style home.

▲ An unassuming plinth block articulates the base of this door jamb.

House Detective

Tim Counts from the Twin Cities Bungalow Club in Minnesota gives a few pointers on the authenticity of painted woodwork: "While Bungalows across the nation share many characteristics, there are also strong regional variables. Look beneath the paint for evidence of stain, varnish, or shellac. You might have to scrape the paint away in an inconspicuous spot and have a professional who knows woodwork and finishes look at the exposed wood." Interior-design books from the early 1900s show a few examples of white painted woodwork, but rarely is it Mission style. Some of these publications, he says, advocated painting woodwork to "brighten up" a room.

◀ From a distance, the room dividers in this 1910 Bungalow appear to be fairly simple. A closer look reveals an intricate classic egg-and-dart pattern that contrasts nicely with the straight grain of the red pine. ▼

Stairs

Considering that most Bungalows were designed as one-story dwellings, there wasn't much emphasis placed on stairs or stair designs. But when it was necessary to include stairs in the design for larger two-story Bungalows, stair design was kept basic and simple. Also, stairs were not prominently featured in the entryways as with Colonials and Victorians but built into areas set back from the front door. This placed a greater emphasis on the living room and eliminated the need for a formal entry hall.

In more mainstream Bungalows, staircases were often split with at least one landing between runs. Staircases found in these period homes typically had plain, unadorned newel posts, balusters, and handrails. Newels, or the posts supporting the handrail at the landing or bottom of the stairs, were generally squared off with a plinth base and top cap. Balusters, or spindle posts, were also squared rather than rounded. Exceptions were seen in houses built by custom builders and in larger Prairie-style examples. Even then, decorative treatments were nominal. For example, a newel might have had a plain bead or row of dentils under the cap. Or there might have been a recessed panel running the length of the post.

▲ The cap of the newel post in this 1915 Bungalow features a complex layering of moldings, giving it a distinctive profile with its pronounced cornice. Classically based dentil molding surrounds the base of the cap.

◄ A newel post on the upstairs landing is simple in its design compared with the one on the first-floor landing. ▼

▶ A conveniently placed built-in seat anchors the stairwell directly opposite the entry in this Prairie-style home.

◀ Quartersawn white oak is perfectly milled for this newly built grand staircase reminiscent of the English Arts and Crafts style. ▲ Baluster designs inspired by the work of 19th-century architect Charles Voysey incorporate custom-made German glass beads to give an otherwise dark staircase illuminating details.

Steps to Safety

If you find yourself having to replace a stairway due to unstable structural support, be sure to contact your local code-enforcement agency. Municipalities require that all new staircases meet specific safety codes, such as riser heights, tread depths, handrail height, and baluster placement to protect against personal injury. Some cities and towns offer exceptions or variances for historic houses, which are determined by the officiating code officer.

▶ The slender balusters in this 1912 Prairie-style home mimic the straight lines of the Mission-style furniture popular at the turn of the 20th century.

 The larger scale of this Mission-style home provides plenty of room for a sweeping staircase.

The simply designed staircases in Bungalow homes are in keeping with the modest lifestyles of their residents. But homes in the Arts and Crafts style were often more grand. Front doors open directly into the living space, setting a casual tone to the interior. Unlike Victorian or Shingle-style homes that feature formal, center staircases, Arts and Crafts staircases shift traffic to the homey living room and fireplace.

◄ Geometric panels are inset into the newel post in this Arts and Crafts–style home. From the time the house was built in 1924, the trimwork was painted, creating a stark contrast to the dark mahogany used in other areas throughout the house.

A Grand Staircase

The homeowners of this newly built Arts and Crafts home liked everything the style had to offer: built-in window seats, inglenooks, and bookcases; an open-plan interior that utilized room dividers to "separate" spaces; and beautiful quartersawn oak woodwork. Once the couple decided to have the house built, their Minneapolis-based architect came up with some inspiring new ideas as well. Leading in from the front porch, a small entry hall diverts traffic in and around a partially concealed staircase.

▲ **A close-up view captures the fine grain of the quarter-sawn oak used in the construction of the staircase skirting.**

Preserving the connection between spaces on the ground floor, the main staircase is built between the entry foyer and dining room with peek-a-boo views into the stairwell. On each side of entry hall and dining room, slender balusters run full height, acting as a screening device between spaces. Light filters through the balusters from both dining-room and entry-hall windows to illuminate the interior of the staircase.

Rich frame-and-panel wainscoting defines the wall space on both sides of the stairwell, anchoring the strong diagonal pattern of the staircase skirting.

Even though the house was a new construction and the homeowners could afford as much space as they needed, they fell in love with the design aesthetic of built-ins inherent to the Arts and Crafts style. It was important to them that their home bore the marks of a craftsman as well.

◀ **A glimpse of the stairwell is seen through tightly spaced balusters upon entering the front door.**

▲ In the dining room, the sharp diagonal lines created by the staircase create
a striking counterpoint to the strict vertical placement of the balusters and high
wainscot wall.

Built-In Furniture

The Bungalow was lauded for its economy in design. Well suited for middle-class families, its compact planning and space-saving innovations such as built-in chests, bookcases, and window seats streamlined the home's interior while providing efficient function.

By constructing the furniture into the design, built-ins kept hallways, bedrooms, and living and dining spaces open and accessible. Their craftsmanship was like fine furniture, following the precepts of honesty and functionality promoted by Morris and Stickley. These pieces were designed to the last detail—the hardware on built-in cabinets, chests, and cupboards, in particular, showcased a meticulous attention to craft.

The built-in designs incorporated many of the same features as the architectural woodwork. Crown moldings topped off cabinets, hutches, and bookcases, while glass fronts mimicked the muntin designs of windows. Even window seats incorporated the same articulation as the wainscoting with recessed or raised panels.

VALUABLE SPACE

The value of built-in furniture has only increased as time has passed, and our 21st-century lifestyles require more and more storage and open space. The thoughtful incorporation of built-ins makes these homes even more desirable in the housing market today. Window seats offer additional storage with hidden compartments beneath, while room dividers separating the living room from the dining room provide cupboard space to store china and tableware. Bookcases double as places to put our slim stereo equipment. Quiet inglenooks provide a perfect place for the family computer.

▲ The china hutch in this 1924 Mission-style home is located in the breakfast nook, which is separated from the dining room by a servant's door. Notice how the glass doors on the hutch match the detailing of the exterior windows.

▲ Many Bungalows featured some sort of built-in furniture framing the fireplace. Here, open bookcases keep a low profile just underneath the mantel.

◀ Room dividers serve as visual boundaries between spaces without fully enclosing the space. These examples in a newly built home feature seethrough lower cabinets fitted with glass shelves. A gently arched opening softens the strict geometry of the columns.

Restoring Built-Ins

Extra care should be taken when restoring original built-ins such as cupboards and cabinets, especially pieces that incorporate leaded or art-glass windows. Since these built-ins integrate delicate hardware and glass details, contact your local historical society to obtain a list of qualified restorers in your area, artisans who specialize in antique-furniture repair.

▲ This new Prairie-style home incorporates some original features such as built-in cabinets flanking the fireplace and a carefully placed window seat in the corner. Wasting no space, a mail sorter is tucked into the side of the cabinet nearest the doorway leading from the living room into a small study.

Room dividers shown here offer plenty of storage for books on the living-room side, while a built-in sideboard on the opposite wall is used as both china cabinet and serving table. The art-glass exterior window details reappear on both the sideboard and room divider bookcases.

Knobs and Pulls

Hardware for built-ins was crafted with the same quality as those used on doors and windows—drawer pulls, handles, and knobs featured designs that incorporated function as well as aesthetics. Designs like the bin pull, pyramid knob, drop pull, or handle latch were fashioned from copper or bronze and finished with an aged patina to give them a more rustic appearance.

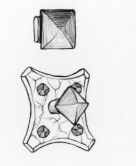

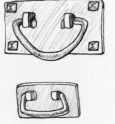

▶ The inglenook in this 1915 Bungalow, with a window seat placed between bookcases, offers a quiet retreat for reading. Bright and sunny, this room now houses the family computer, where the homeowner's three children gather to do their homework.

◀ In this large Mission-style home, the room divider between living and dining areas features built-in bookcases with leaded-glass detailing.

▶ Creative planning places a cozy built-in window seat in the living-room corner of a new Prairie home. Outfitted with drawers that easily slide in and out on metal glides, the window seat provides storage for family puzzles and games.

▶ When this dining room was expanded to accommodate a larger kitchen, a built-in sideboard was designed to match the glass and hardware to the home's existing room divider. The architects integrated the leaded-glass doors from the original ▲ into the newly-built sideboard. Hardware was matched to the original, and the homeowners decided to allow the patina to age over time.

▶ Most often, master bedrooms in Bungalow style interiors had some sort of built-ins. This early example from 1899 features a built-in wardrobe closet, cabinet with drawers, and a door that opens to a built-in sink.

◀ A Mission-style home from 1930 has a built-in china cabinet located in the breakfast room. Unlike modest Bungalow styles, this home maintained servants' quarters. The breakfast room acted as a butler's pantry during formal dinners. In keeping with the style, the stained-glass doors on the hutch mimic the arch of the recess above.

THREE

Interior Details

THE ARTS AND CRAFTS MOVEMENT created a rich aesthetic that focused on honest, unadorned materials, on a particular simplicity of design, and on nature itself as a subject for celebration. As a result, the plain yet beautiful interior details of Arts and Crafts and Bungalow homes may just be the best expression of the movement's style in handicrafts.

These handsomely finished rooms radiated warmth because one could actually see the materials. Exposed wood adorned floors and ceilings and wall paneling, all of it striking for the vivid pattern of its grain—not for ornate carving that dominated earlier styles. Clay tiles decorated fireplaces and hearths.

And the natural materials created pleasing texture variations throughout. Smooth paneling offered a subtle contrast against the coarseness of hand-troweled plaster walls, while sleek stained door panels with beveled glass complemented hand-forged metal hardware. Honest tile, stone, and brick—honest because they were presented in their natural, unadulterated states—accented fireplaces and floors.

Contrasting colors also added to the visual intensity of Bungalow interiors. Earth tones enriched wallpaper patterns. Painted plaster walls deepened the appearance of wood that was stained dark. These natural materials were layered, which further contributed to the beauty of the rooms.

Bungalow style subtly integrated animal and plant imagery in keeping with the Arts and Crafts movement's focus on all things natural. Period wallpapers and stencil designs

◀ **A study in contrasts, this library space is dressed up with white wall paneling and a painted window seat, while the broad display shelf supported by small brackets remind of the more rustic hand-craftsmanship employed. Photo © www.carolyn-bates.com, Sandra Vitzthum Architect, LLC.**

featured delicate and colorful renderings of flora and fauna. Ceramic tile surrounds also featured stylized natural representations.

By design, these homes had open floor plans and were built both in modest proportion as well as on a grand scale. As with any space, incorporating too many details into a small area can make a room look crowded. Of course, a room with too few details leaves it feeling bare or somber. So it was important to create visual patterns in these open floor plans by reiterating finish materials from room to room. This way, flow for the whole interior was established.

Arts and Crafts and Bungalow homes worked because the details worked. When lost or damaged details have been replaced and a house is successfully restored, the design feels right. The proportions are pleasing, and the finish materials are in harmony. The space feels welcoming, intimate, and expansive at the same time.

▲ A major renovation involved matching woodwork and wainscoting to the original remnants of detailing and adding a frieze whose pattern was inspired by William Morris wallpaper. The result is a cozy corner retreat.

◄ The owners decided to expand the living space in their Prairie style home by enclosing the outside porch. Exposed brick walls create a counterpoint to the concrete ceiling, while the quarry-tile floor is softened by an area rug.

▲ **Wainscoting made from quartersawn oak has developed a dark, rich patina over the years. The profile of the wainscoting cap was derived from the proportions of the crown molding.**

LEAVING ROOM FOR PERSONAL TASTE

A careful renovation or building a new house always allows room for a homeowner to make a personal statement. When selecting interior finish materials such as wallpaper, paint colors, ceiling materials, and flooring, think about the general architecture to a point.

These details should underline a defined style about the whole house. You may own a rustic or early example of the style, a vernacular or more common example, or a high-end or formal example. In this chapter, you'll be able to find ideas relating to each of these types of Bungalows. But no matter how you make over or design your home, it goes without saying that any work should incorporate your personal taste.

IN HISTORY

William Morris (1834–1896), the innovative force of the Arts and Crafts movement, introduced Victorian England to quality handcrafted furnishings. His designs were reminiscent of those produced by medieval craft guilds. His firm of architects, artists, and furniture makers, called Morris & Co., designed wallpapers, textiles, and furniture, which offered clients a completely unified interior scheme. Morris's philosophy that one should "have nothing in your house which you do not know to be useful or believe to be beautiful" represented a major departure from designing with heavy ornament, which was so popular among his fellow Victorians.

Wallpaper in the pomegranate fruit pattern designed by Morris appears above the lincrusta wainscoting in a room furnished with Sussex chairs from Morris and Co.

Finishing Touches

I T WAS A CHALLENGE TO SELECT finish materials for this new Arts and Crafts–style home that were sensitive to the period and maintained the flow of space from one room to the next. Contrasting flooring such as the limestone tiles and quartersawn oak seen here separate rooms into their distinctive functions. The limestone serves as a durable material for hallways, while wood floors warm the dining and living rooms.

Matched wainscot walls connect hallways and direct traffic flow between spaces, while the cased openings trimmed in the same dark wood created a rhythmic pattern on corridor walls. Unifying the scheme, the designer chose to treat the walls with a polished-wax method utilized by Gustav Stickley in his Craftsman homes.

The plaster was stenciled with a light blue floral pattern, then several layers of wax, each buffed to a matte sheen, were applied to create tonal contrasts.

Ceiling beams balance the visual weight of wainscoting and flooring from area to area. Hallways incorporate simple running beams that span the width of each corridor. The dining room features a complete ceiling grid of boxed beams, which enhances the visual dominance of the wood floor and furniture.

▲ Dark stain applied to the woodwork in the dining room offers a striking contrast to the paleness of the walls.

◄ A soft blue and light cream stencil design is buffed with several layers of wax to give the plaster a matte sheen.

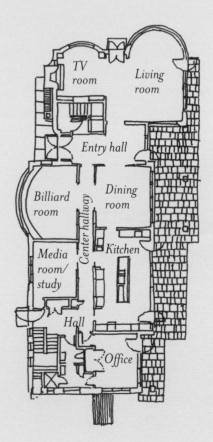

▲ This new dining room showcases interior finishes inspired by Arts and Crafts designers at the turn of the 20th century.

Wall Treatments

To compensate for the modest scale of most Bungalows, much attention was paid to the interiors—and the walls in particular. Beautiful quartersawn oak, red pine, elm, fir, or gum was used for wall paneling and wainscoting. Also, these walls showcased stenciling, painted plaster, and new designs in wallpaper, creating innovative decorative effects.

Wall panels continued to reflect Victorian influences in that they were designed with narrow stiles and rails, which framed sunken panels. In living and dining rooms, these panels were sometimes capped with a chair rail wide enough to display contemporary pottery. Regional influences and budget restrictions determined the types of wood used for the wainscoting. Quartersawn oak was installed in high-end interiors. For more modest homes, paneling was made from gumwood or red pine.

▲ Reclaimed attic space provides the perfect setting for a home office, which features recessed-panel wainscoting, oak strip flooring, and broad crown molding.

The Chauncey frieze wall covering accentuates the continuous line of trimwork that surrounds the windows and overmantel, lending balance to a room with a very high ceiling.

▼ Named for an original owner of the house in Marshall, Michigan, where the paper was found, this gentle meander design, "Chauncy Frieze," dates from c. 1880–90. Its pattern and earth tone coloration is still a popular choice for homeowners of today.

IN HISTORY

Gustav Stickley launched his magazine *The Craftsman* in 1901, introducing the American public to his vision for a housing style based on integrated exteriors and interiors. Designs featured included uncomplicated interiors with clean lines, plaster walls, and exposed beams. *The Craftsman* offered scaled house plans that served as the background for Stickley's furniture designs.

▶ Running the perimeter of this living room, a taller-than-average wainscoting successfully integrates a heavy cap, and its vertical panels complement the trim design used around both doors and windows.

▲ Frame-and-panel-construction wall paneling breaks the wall surface into a grid pattern, offering a buffer between banquette seating and the high bookshelves and display ledge.

Plaster finishes varied from region to region. In the South and Southwest, the popular Mission style emphasized the coarseness of the plaster. This highly textured surface was often painted in earth-tone colors. When light played across the wall plane, the resulting shadows created a fuller, more three-dimensional quality.

In the Midwest and Northeast, plaster walls were generally smoother but featured equally dramatic results. By layering contrasting colors or subtle tones over one another, then sealing the plaster with a tinted glaze coat or wax, this plaster treatment produced its own visual display. This trapped and reflected light between the layer of wall and the glaze, giving depth to the color.

Stencil designs focusing on geometric patterns or wild botanicals were typical Arts and Crafts designs. A touch that was done by hand, stenciling added rustic decoration and was a quick and inexpensive alternative to wallpaper.

The wallpapers of the period remain striking today. Modeled after designs from the English Arts and Crafts movement, bold floral patterns in dark colors with light patterned accents combined with coordinating borders to decorate the walls of bedrooms, dining rooms, and foyers.

▲ The Craftsman Bungalow bedroom is light and airy with its painted wood-work and simple detailing. The picture-molding area is transformed with a hand-stenciled spade design adapted from a 1905 copy of *The Craftsman*.

Uniformity

For rooms where architectural details such as moldings, varying window heights, or unusual ceiling treatments break up the continuity, painting walls and ceilings in light colors or in the same color helps unify the space and keep the eye focused on the furnishings and accessories. Selecting paint colors for millwork details such as window and door trim, crown moldings, and baseboards that blend with the wall and ceiling colors enhance the effect.

▲ The cathedral ceiling in this Mission home is articulated by intricate plasterwork and Moorish pendants. The home's recessed niches, Moorish arches, and rough stucco walls all speak to its Spanish Mission influence.

◄ Faux finishing creates a sense of depth on the walls in this Prairie breakfast room. Visual texture is achieved by layering orange tones with rollers and sponges over the base color.

A New Billiard Room

THE ARCHITECTS CREATED A MASCULINE FEEL in this billiard room by emphasizing the mass and scale of the room's walls, ceilings, window trim, and floors. Quartersawn white oak in a rich, honey finish unifies the interior details, carefully balancing its weight against the oversized pool table. Softening the formality of the wood, a 360-degree mural created by a team of artists graces the upper frieze area of the walls. Inspired by the beauty of Martha's Vineyard, where the home is located, the artists incorporated beach plum trees and local flora and fauna in their scheme.

The outside view of beach plum trees is captured in a mural in this billiards room. The soft colors and styling of the trees are modeled after the work of English Arts and Crafts muralists.

◀ This elaborate ceiling was hung with faux gilded burlap and the beams outlined with "Apple Tree Border," circa 1910. Matching patterns, "Apple Tree Frieze" and "Apple Tree Border," fill the area above the picture rail. The walls were hung with a leaf pattern, "Glenwood," to complete the interior scheme. ▼

▲ "The Stag" depicts an enchanted landscape, an artist's vision of a royal English park, abstracted and stylized in the design tradition of the Arts and Crafts movement. This wallpaper pattern was introduced in 1896 by C. F. A. Voysey in *The Studio*.

▲ This wallpaper, a meander of foliage counterpointed by a grid of flowers, is a fine homage to William Morris, whose lush designs of the late 19th century embodied the Arts and Crafts movement.

▶ Heavily textured embossed wall covering was used in original Bungalow and Arts and Crafts interiors. Lincrusta (at right) and anaglypta wallpapers, developed in the late 1800s, offered the look of tooled leather.

Original Beauty

THE OWNERS OF THIS ARTS AND CRAFTS home in Spokane, Wash., chose to turn this alcove space off the living room into a cozy sitting area. Original multiple panel insets in the high wainscot wall create a definitive grid pattern, mimicking the window muntins. After finding the original anaglypta wallpaper set within each wainscot panel intact, the homeowners decided to sponge-paint the frieze and ceiling in a soft parchment color to enhance the visual texture of the wall covering. Wicker furniture serves as an appealing textural counterpoint to the smoothness of the quartersawn oak of moldings and floors.

A small alcove off the main entry serves as a reading room in this Craftsman-style Bungalow.

Arts and Crafts Wallpaper

Larger Arts and Crafts–style interiors combined geometric borders with free-form botanical patterns within the same room, often gracing walls and ceilings. In smaller-scaled Bungalows, wallpapers were used in combination with paint or often appeared as accents in the upper frieze. In the early 20th century, when wallpaper was no longer hand-blocked but mass-produced, it became more affordable to middle-class homeowners.

This border paper shows a stylized view into a forest.

▲ Abstracted in the manner of the finest Arts and Crafts designs, this botanical pattern has an elegance that is underscored by the simple use of color.

▲ A late 19th-century wallpaper designed in the manner of Morris & Co. is reproduced today and available in four colors: century red (above), soft green, butterscotch, and terra cotta.

▶ The bold color and pattern from this Arts and Crafts–period reproduction wallpaper enhance the richness of an antique sideboard made from quartersawn oak. Photo © www.carolynbates.com, Sandra Vitzthum Architect, LLC.

▲ A botanical-patterned wallpaper in soft yellows and cream complements the intricate marquetry design in this Eastlake headboard, a style popular in the late 1800s. ▶ Photo © www.carolynbates.com, Sandra Vitzthum Architect, LLC.

Arts and Crafts or Glasgow Rose?

There are many rose designs that appear on Arts and Crafts wallpapers, furniture prints, objets, and glazing. Most are stylized, often graphic in character with a flatness that abstracts the shape. Although many Arts and Crafts designers have used

the motif in their work, Charles Rennie Mackintosh and Dard Hunter are most notable.

Mackintosh's roses are integrated into some of his earliest drawings and furniture designs dating back to 1902. The name "Glasgow rose" is taken from the Glasgow School of Art in Scotland where Mackintosh studied. During his tenure, he formed a partnership with Herbert McNair, and the two met and married fellow students, Margaret and Frances MacDonald. "The Four," as they were known, designed furniture, artwork, and tableware for a successful chain of tea rooms throughout Glasgow. The "Glasgow rose" is featured in many of these designs.

American Dard Hunter began using the rose pattern in the work he created for Roycroft Studios. Dubbed the "Arts and Crafts rose," the motif was used on a variety of objects ranging from stained-glass windows to ceramic vases.

▲ A refreshing change from painted walls, this California Bungalow bedroom is decorated with three types of wall covering. A simple stripe accents the headboard and balances the height of the neighboring window, while Glasgow roses are used in combination with panels and frieze borders.

Arts and Crafts Color

▼ The rough surface texture of the plaster walls is enhanced by a faux finishing technique that involves layering three shades of yellow with paint rollers and sponges.

By the turn of the 20th century, Americans had long been decorating with dark colors and bold patterns, which were featured in Victorian houses. The deep burgundy and dark forest-green hues found in 19th-century homes harmonized with warm tones of the woodwork. This tradition of rich color carried over to the new Bungalow style in varying degrees. Deep burgundy was replaced with bright terra cotta, while forest green became lighter in tone and intensity, producing the delicate sage green associated today with the Arts and Crafts aesthetic.

When remodeling, the easiest thing to do is repaint your walls, but before you purchase that first gallon, take the time to know the history. Color palettes come and go just like the fashions of the day. The most successful Bungalow renovations are done by homeowners who have a general idea of the colors that were commonly found in them. Since Bungalows are popular again, it's not difficult to find which palettes are appropriate for a home today. Major paint manufacturers offer historic selections categorized by style or era. And they can recommend combinations that include colors for exteriors and interiors and coordinate colors for trim, walls, and ceilings.

The second part of the color equation is personal taste. After gathering a general knowledge of the historically accurate color schemes, most homeowners ask themselves which hues match their lifestyle and the modesty or formality of their particular home.

Use these palettes as a guideline for selecting period-appropriate colors for your vintage-style home.

Handicraft Hues

Fan decks supplied by paint manufacturers make it easy to customize paints for your home. These color tiles show the range of values, or intensities, for each color on the same paint strip. This is a helpful tool in seeing just how dark or light tones within the same range might work together for your space. But the historical color palette is just the basis for getting started.

Each color can be adjusted to match your taste and lifestyle. For example, sage green may be historically appropriate, but you may discover that a cleaner and lighter celadon actually works better for your interior—mostly because you like it better.

▲ The same paint color is used in the dining room, center hallway, and living room to maintain a visual flow between the living spaces.

Color Effects

Although dark colors have a tendency to make rooms look smaller, they also can make the room feel more intimate and cozy. In addition, a dark background provides a nice contrast to architectural details if your vintage house has painted millwork such as doors, trim, and moldings. And since natural and artificial lighting affect color in different ways, a dark room can feel light and vibrant in the daytime, yet quiet and sophisticated at night under the warmth of incandescent lighting.

▼ Earth colors like these were a common feature of Bungalow homes at the turn of the 20th century. A unique combination pairing pepper-red walls with sun-drenched-yellow ceiling punctuates the interior of this breakfast nook. By painting the ceiling and the upper frieze the same color, the room appears larger.

▲ This soft buff paint color enhances the warmth of the wood trim and built-in unit in this Arts and Crafts–style kitchen. The same color, two shades darker, lines the interiors of the cabinets under the transom, adding more depth to the recessed area and accentuating the collection of pottery.

Start Small

Once you're ready to begin experimenting with color, start small. Get a quart of paint, and test it until you get the right value or tone. You might want a yellow kitchen, but a subtle buttercup yellow may suit your lifestyle better than a playful sunshine yellow.

Test the color on a wall next to a window during daylight hours. Placing the hue next to a window reveals the color under filtered light rather than under direct sunlight. Next, paint a large enough area to see the contrast against the trim, and look at the color through the day and under the artificial light at night. Remember, a small paint chip from a fan deck may not read the same way when magnified on four walls.

Ceilings

Often overlooked but important in the grand scheme of things, the fifth plane—the ceiling—has a profound effect on how we experience our interior space. Too high and we feel small; too low and we feel confined.

Ceilings were given the same careful consideration as the walls and floors, unlike many of today's newer home designs. While Mission homes incorporated highly vaulted ceilings, most Prairie houses and Bungalows had 8-ft. to 9-ft. ceilings, which by emphasizing the horizontal plane made the ceilings feel lower. To counter this effect, molding placed two-thirds up the wall—typically a narrow bead—gave the illusion of a higher ceiling.

Ceilings in Bungalows could be handsomely decorated. Boxed beams, running beams, or geometrically arranged moldings sectioned off the ceiling's surface and were often adorned with wallpaper or colorful paints. These visual additions expanded the sense of scale, too. Tongue-and-groove paneling, which was originally installed on porch ceilings, appeared in kitchens, bathrooms, and enclosed sleeping porches.

The use of plasterwork and plaster moldings varies significantly from region to region. Although plasterwork wasn't the norm, in the Southwest, for example, crown moldings from cast plaster were popular. Early Prairies featured ceiling medallions.

▶ Narrow strips of oak create a grid around large structural beams in this Prairie-style home and unify each of the design elements, which reflect a heavy Frank Lloyd Wright influence.

◄ At the top of the entry stairwell, a pair of trusses inspired by the work of Charles Rennie Mackintosh support a skylighted ridge. The skylight brings natural light into the stairwell below, illuminating small glass beads set into each baluster.

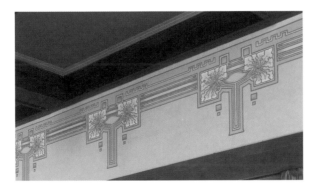

▲ Frieze panels of geometric-patterned wallpaper direct the eyes toward the ceiling, drawing attention to the heavily proportioned beams. The grid of the ceiling beams is accentuated by a thin wallpaper border in a patterned stripe. ▼

▲ The architect of this newly built Arts and Crafts home opted for skylights instead of plaster and wood beams in this upstairs hallway. The horizontal panels break up the length of the hallway while flooding the space with natural light.

Stamp of Approval

Metal ceiling tiles developed in the mid-19th century were a more economical replacement to the fancy plasterwork ceiling designs found in Victorian homes. Machinery paved the way for mass production of metal tiles by the end of the century. Designs were pressed into tin or, in some cases, into copper by using stamp presses.

The popularity of metal ceilings peaked in the 1890s, just as some of the earliest Bungalows were built. The fire-resistant nature of the material made it a desirable ceiling treatment in kitchens. During World War I, production was curtailed so the much-needed metal could be used for the war effort.

The tin ceiling in this 1915 Bungalow was replaced with a highly textured reproduction design, which offers a sharp contrast to the tongue-and-groove paneling on the walls.

◄ Beams made from feather-grain mahogany lead the eye upward to the slightly pitched ceiling in this Southern California den. The room predominantly incorporates a mix of mahogany and oak in the architectural elements.

▶ Ceiling beams in a running pattern enhance the woodwork around doors and windows in this dining room. The beams are largely decorative; their massive scale mirrors the weight of the crown molding, enhancing the visual flow from dining room to kitchen.

Plasterwork

Decorative plasterwork on ceilings was less popular during the Arts and Crafts era; it's a holdover from Victorian times that found its way into some of the more elaborate Bungalows of the period. Plasterwork was better suited to the Mission-style Bungalows, offering a pleasant contrast to the heavy texture of stucco walls. Plaster medallions based on Moorish and Christian themes popular in the Spanish missions were shaped in molds.

A stylized grape cluster and vine pattern, symbols of the Eucharist, appears in the plaster ceiling molding in this Mission-style Bungalow from 1930.

▶ White ceiling beams harmonize with the trim and window muntins in this restored Arts and Crafts–style home. Painted woodwork became more the mode in Bungalows in the 1920s, borrowing from the recently introduced Neo-Colonial style.

▼ This grand Mission-style home built in 1924 incorporates painted woodwork, reflecting a new formality in the Arts and Crafts aesthetic. Stark white molding, trim, and built-ins surround folding doors that separate the living and dining spaces.

Floors

Flooring in Arts and Crafts and Bungalow homes relied heavily on wood strips in oak, red or yellow pine, and fir. In the main areas of the house, floorboards varied in width, depending on the type of wood. Narrow, 1-in. strips of wood, called matchstick flooring, are more often found in sleeping porches or on outside porches. The matchstick flooring provided a pleasing visual balance to the tongue-and-groove ceilings that typically graced these spaces.

Although one may think of hardwood as the quintessential flooring material for these homes, by the 1920s, a greater variety of flooring choices had been introduced. Tile, stone, brick, and even linoleum appeared in bathrooms, entryways, and kitchens. Other flooring materials such as brick and quarry tile became common choices for hearths and entryways.

The impervious quality of ceramic tile made it an ideal choice for bathrooms. Meant for use on floors and walls, ceramic-tile designs incorporated an array of shapes and colors in Bungalow bathrooms.

Heavily influenced by the Mission-style, mosaic flooring found its way into bathrooms and entryways, as well as to outside areas of porches and patios. Whether broken tiles or small 1-in. tiles in varying shapes of solid hue, mosaic tiles brought color and pattern to otherwise ordinary floors.

▼ Strip flooring in golden oak was laid with borders that separate and define connecting spaces. The floor takes you from the dining room, past the entryway, and into the living room beyond.

▲ Durable brick flooring in this entryway takes the brunt
of the weather, heavy traffic, and hard use, protecting the
wood flooring in the living room.

◀ The common practice of using tile on floors today is probably the biggest design contribution of the Mission style. Here, pentagonal-shaped tile creates an attractive pattern when matched with smaller mosaic pieces in the same color scheme.

▶ The mosaic floor in the entry hall of this Mission-style Bungalow is a hardy and beautiful buffer from the outside elements. With a hexagonal tile perimeter, shards of decorative and field tile create a colorful random design.

▲ The sleeping porch in this newly built Arts and Crafts–style home uses redwood flooring, which stands up well to humidity and moisture. The hardwood strips echo the linearity of the thin matchstick strips of the tongue-and-groove ceiling.

Enduring Floors

ALTHOUGH LINOLEUM IS ASSOCIATED with post-World War II suburban living, the flooring material has been available since the mid-19th century. Made from all-natural materials such as linseed oil, wood or cork fillers, and plant resins, early linoleum has proven to be a durable floor covering, lasting 40 years or more.

Its popularity waned in the 1970s as the cheaper vinyl flooring became more widely available. Today, linoleum's popularity has returned, not only because the retro designs are appealing to younger homeowners but also because many linoleum products are manufactured using environmentally safe materials.

When homeowners Stephanie Pollack and Ken Snow remodeled their 1917 Bungalow kitchen, they replaced the old linoleum floor. The new linoleum uses a narrow contrasting band of color along the perimeter that unifies the workspace with the breakfast table.

◀ The random diamond pattern of this contemporary linoleum floor connects the flow of space between the butler's pantry and kitchen.

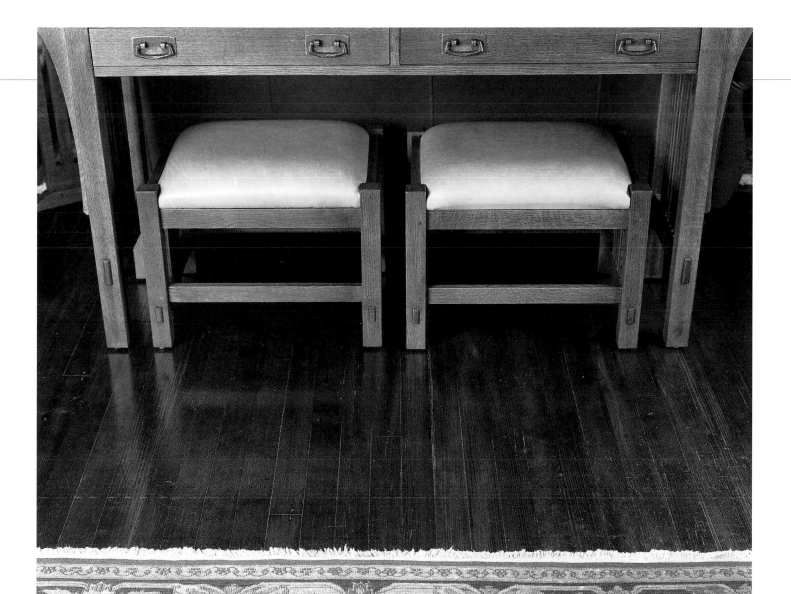

William Morris loved to weave. He created designs from scratch, mixing his own dyes to get just the right color for the yarns. His favorite motifs focused on organic forms, including flowers, birds, and vine patterns, which were interpreted into vivid colors in his woven and printed designs. Morris's residence, Kelmscott House, in Hammersmith, England, is full of his wallpapers, furniture, carpets, and fabrics. Today, the home stands as a tribute to Morris's career as an artist and designer. The "Hammersmith" collection at Kelmscott is a museum open to the public.

▲ Original quartersawn oak floors are protected by a large area rug placed underneath heavy furniture. The rug's decorative pattern was inspired by the botanicals found in wallpaper designs of the Arts and Crafts period.

FOUR

Finding and Creating Space

OR THOSE FORTUNATE ENOUGH to own—and update—an Arts and Crafts– or Bungalow-style home today, finding enough space for living and storage is usually the biggest challenge. The open layout of earlier Bungalows can be easily adapted to today's lifestyle. But these old homes were built in a time before television sets, computers, and microwave ovens, so it should be no surprise that often there just isn't enough room for the stuff of modern living.

In addition to storage, people today require larger rooms. There's a high priority placed on convenience and comfort, and lifestyle habits have changed. We spend much time in the kitchen and family room, for example. It's rare that the classic Bungalow—or most any antique home—offers the space needed to accommodate these needs. Bungalows, for example, rarely had more than one bathroom.

It's a creative feat to add on to or reconfigure living space without sacrificing the rhythm and scale of the historic style. But it can be done. One solution is to take down walls or closets. Another is to build a new addition.

Although usually a tremendous undertaking, adding on to the original house for many homeowners is the most direct solution for gaining more space. But this is where most design mistakes are made. Updating a small kitchen or adding a much needed master bedroom, bath, and closet must be done with a careful eye to the overall style of the house.

It's important to be realistic about budget, time, and available resources and to think about what any such project will add to the value of the home. An experienced design professional knows how to ensure homeowners get what they need while maintaining the integrity of the home.

◄ A new addition designed to keep with the home's Prairie style accommodates a gourmet kitchen, inglenook, and breakfast room. ► In finer homes, the butler's pantry provided a buffer space between the kitchen and dining room for serving the evening meal. Photo © www.carolyn-bates.com, Sandra Vitzthum Architect, LLC.

▶ This original Bungalow kitchen is typical of the style: It's small to accommodate one cook. Crisp, white kitchen cabinets are a pleasant contrast to warm wood flooring and countertops. Casement windows, another key component, bring in natural light and fresh air. True-to-the-period pendant lights with Holophane glass shades illuminate the space at night.

▲ Although lacking the modern improvements, the original plumbing fixtures in this period home were deemed by the owners to be too precious to replace. Photo © www.carolynbates.com, Sandra Vitzthum Architect, LLC.

▲ Today's manufacturers make the task of selecting appropriately designed Arts and Crafts cabinets easier by offering a wide selection of period-inspired styles. This kitchen is set up with a split work surface for preparing pastries. The lowered section makes it easier to roll out pastry, and the marble countertop keeps the dough from sticking to the surface.

▲ A new family room and eat-in kitchen accommodate today's casual entertaining style by keeping the space open and connected. Arts and Crafts styling is expressed in the tall wainscot wall with its wide cap and sunken panels, wood lath on the ceiling, and high plate rack running the length of the cased opening between rooms. Photo © www.carolynbates.com, Sandra Vitzthum Architect, LLC.

Kitchens

The earliest Arts and Crafts and Bungalow kitchens were designed to accommodate a cook or a maid. All meals were eaten in the dining room. Today, many kitchens are renovated or replaced completely with regard to modern convenience and technology. But when there's little attention paid to the home's intrinsic aesthetic (and even though the homeowner may have spent lots of money on the new kitchen), this renovation may detract from the home's value.

There is hardly a thing called a minor project when updating the kitchen is involved, whether a museum-like renovation, a more mainstream project, or a very high-end redo is the goal. It takes planning and guidance—and research. By selecting the right combination of cabinetry and hardware designs, countertop materials, and appliances, a Bungalow kitchen can be redesigned with sensitivity to the house's history.

▼ A redesigned eat-in kitchen maintains elements of Bungalow styling with its old-fashioned enameled cooking stove, bin-pull hardware, and built-in inglenook. Modern conveniences such as the dishwasher and television are close to area workspaces.

▲ Where nostalgia and modern amenity meet: Cabinetry and hardware replicate styles of the early 1900s, while hardwood floors and stainless steel with butcher-block countertops complete the historic scheme.

Kitchen Counsel

If building a new addition is the only way to accommodate a much-needed kitchen and your home is located in a historic district, start by contacting your local landmarks commission to obtain guidelines for making alterations. This will save you, your architect, and general contractor valuable time and trouble by learning the parameters of the city or village ordinances.

MATERIALS AND APPLIANCES

Individual taste, budget, and performance all come into play when selecting materials and appliances for your new kitchen. Handmade tile typical of Prairie and Craftsman styles, with their richly embossed surfaces, are beautiful to look at but hard to maintain. For example, slate countertops may be appealing at first, but the stone, which stains over time, will develop a natural patina very different from its original condition. This may not look so good after all.

Concerning cabinetry, many design professionals take cues from original woodwork details throughout the house. Quartersawn oak seen in an inglenook, for example, might also be used in kitchen cabinetry.

Appliances and fixtures are available in a wide array of styles from farm sinks to porcelain-handled faucets, making the job a lot easier for homeowners. In today's design market, there are many appropriate choices that fit nearly any price range.

▲ A new kitchen conveys Arts and Crafts styling with oak cabinets custom-made to imitate the detailing of the wainscoting. The cabinetry's high-end look incorporates brushed-nickel hardware accents and glass-fronted upper cabinets. Recessed halogens inside the upper cabinets keep the design bright.

Architect or Interior Designer?

If your home requires structural changes, as when building an addition, you should hire an architect to prepare the drawings. And when the job doesn't call for moving or knocking down walls, degree-holding interior designers can address many space-planning issues, as well as help in the selection of interior finish materials. Both an architect and an interior designer can prepare drawings and provide specifications in order to procure bids from contractors.

Since regulations regarding licensing vary from state to state, start by checking with your local zoning and planning commission to find out who can obtain the necessary building permits. Often, a builder or interior designer can stand in for an architect, which might be the case if you've hired one or both already for another aspect of the job.

Architects and interior designers with expertise in Arts and Crafts– or Bungalow-style homes can be found by contacting these professional organizations: the American Institute of Architects, the American Society of Interior Designers, and the International Interior Design Association.

▲ Inspired by a Stickley-designed breakfast set, this sideboard conveys the style with custom cabinetry that's matched to the wall paneling.

From Porch to Pantry

W HEN STEPHANIE POLLACK and husband Ken
Snow decided to update the kitchen and master
bedroom in their 1917 Bungalow in Newton, Mass.,
they had specific requirements. Since both are pursu-
ing careers, at-home time with their three children
and extended family played an important part in the
design planning.

By converting the home's original sleeping porches
into interior space, the family gained an eat-in
kitchen, butler's pantry, and mudroom complete with
plenty of storage downstairs. Upstairs, two sleeping
porches were combined to create a master suite with
closets, a dressing area, and a bathroom.

▲ The interior of this 1917 Craftsman Bungalow got a
makeover, while the footprint and the facade remained
unchanged.

Before

After

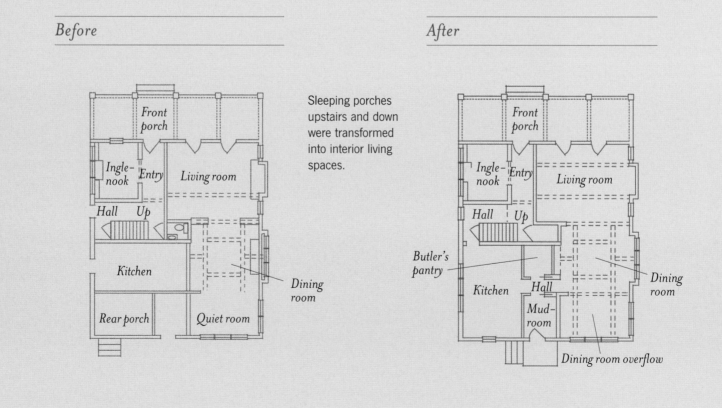

Sleeping porches
upstairs and down
were transformed
into interior living
spaces.

◄ A group of windows was added to provide a clear view into the side yard from the breakfast table. The cross-lattice design in the upper sash mimics original windows found in the inglenook.

Careful consideration in matching original elements from the front porch, such as exposed rafters, tongue-and-groove ceiling, and porch posts, was used in the design of the new back porch leading into the mud-room. The mudroom opens to a butler's pantry that separates the kitchen from the dining space.

Because the family keeps a kosher kitchen, they require two dishwashers, two ovens, and plenty of storage for separate meat and dairy prep areas. Custom kitchen cabinetry runs to the ceiling for additional storage. Glass in the doors of the upper cabinets creates a showcase for colorful Arts and Crafts–style pottery.

▲ A butler's pantry with tongue-and-groove paneling located off the hallway from the mud-room separates the kitchen from the dining room.

▲ Multiple work zones in this eat-in kitchen provide enough space for more than one cook. A reconditioned stove captures the romance of an earlier time, while a combination of beadboard and recessed-panel cabinetry sets the Arts and Crafts theme.

▶ A grand kitchen designed for a new Arts and Crafts home features state-of-the-art amenities such as a Sub-Zero® refrigerator, Viking® six-burner stove, Gröhe® faucets, and porcelain farm sink. Bench-built cabinetry made from quartersawn white oak captures the style with its frame-and-panel fronts, while illuminated bottle glass accents upper cabinets.

Gourmet Style

A NEW ADDITION GAVE THIS MINNESOTA family enough space for a cook's kitchen, a sizeable breakfast nook, and a separate butler's pantry. Millwork details borrowed from the original 1917 Prairie-style home were incorporated into the kitchen cabinetry and ceiling design. Lighting fixtures and clerestory windows placed high above the cabinets contain colorful art glass and look as though they could have been designed by Frank Lloyd Wright.

▲ Fashioned into a classic Prairie-style grid pattern, a wooden screen filters natural light from a window in the home-office alcove into the kitchen.

▼ A kitchen island offers extra workspace that features a practical vegetable sink. Handy storage below includes a wine rack and pull-out bins. A Sub-Zero refrigerator is cleverly concealed behind wood panels.

▲ A warming oven in the island is conveniently positioned directly across from the stove.

▲ Besides the high-end finish materials (mahogany cabinets and paneling and slate sink and countertop), this kitchen design is classic. In this 1917 Bungalow redo, African mahogany was found in the dining room, so the new paneling was designed to match. Copper hardware and a period-inspired pendant light fixture are reproductions that update the look perfectly.

▲ While updating this Prairie-style kitchen, the homeowners opted to hide the refrigerator and dishwasher behind wood panels to blend with the cabinetry.

Out of Sight

Dishwashers, double ovens, and refrigerators, not to mention small appliances such as blenders, microwaves, and food processors, need to be accessible yet remain unobtrusive. These days, you can conceal the refrigerator and dishwasher doors behind paneling. When it comes to counter space for other appliances, plan extra areas in cupboards, and add appliance garages so these items can be stowed away.

◄ Clearly a solution worth waiting for, this new addition combines breakfast area, kitchen, and family room in one unified block of space. Gray granite countertops blend with the sleek stainless steel of modern appliances, while brass hardware accentuates Arts and Crafts–style cabinets. The glazed upper cabinets with four-over-two muntin spacing maintain a rhythmic flow inspired by window patterns seen throughout the house.

▲ A seamless, honed granite countertop and stainless steel sink with retro faucets offer a practical solution to this work island. Unlike soapstone, honed (not polished) granite is much easier to maintain because it doesn't stain as easily.

▲ A 1920s kitchen features a porcelain sink, chrome faucet with porcelain handles, and recessed porcelain soap holders. A thin border of black and green tile enhances the unique color of the original subway tile. Completing the authenticity of the period kitchen, new cabinets and a linoleum floor mimic period designs.

◀ In addition to the colorful tilework in this Mission-style Bungalow, the sink and countertop in the butler's pantry are made from nickel silver. Before stainless steel became widely available, nickel silver, more sanitary than wood, was the predominant surfacing material.

Kitchen Convenience

Not ones to shy away from hard work, the new owners of this Bungalow jumped when they saw it advertised as a fixer-upper. Fire and pest damage spelled gut renovation for their prize, a 1912 Bungalow, so they demolished it down to the studs. Starting with a clean slate presented a great opportunity for them to reconfigure the downstairs to make better use of the space. The old area, which included a mudroom and pantry, was combined to create a large, new kitchen with boothlike banquettes. The balance between old and new features, not an uncommon hurdle for those making renovations, is worked out perfectly here with a warm, traditional color palette and both modern and reproduction appliances.

Making the most of their situation, the owners created a laundry space in the kitchen area that is nicely camouflaged in a large closet. No more hauling loads of laundry up and down basement stairs—the new washer and dryer are hidden behind new oak five-panel doors.

▲ After a total renovation, this once dilapidated 1912 Bungalow in the Seattle area was transformed into a beauty.

▲ By reconfiguring the kitchen, the owners were able to add space while maintaining the house's classic open plan.

◀ A full laundry center is kept out of sight behind oak doors that echo the simple, honest design of the kitchen cabinetry. Shelving above the washer and dryer keeps cleaning supplies handy.

Restoration Hardware

RATHER THAN REPLACE THEIR 1910 BUNGALOW kitchen with a newer one, Barbara and Glenn Avery decided to go to work on what they already had. They stripped layers of paint from the cabinets, soaked the hardware in solvents to loosen years of grime, sanded and refinished the butcher-block countertop along with the original hardwood floors, and installed a new tin ceiling. The project took several months, but now the couple once more enjoys the authentic beauty of a kitchen that's a hundred years old.

▲ Instead of replacing all of the kitchen hardware, the Averys decided to clean the original bin-pull handles and latches.

▼ One change to this otherwise original kitchen is the glazing added to the front panels of the upper cabinets, which add reflectivity and light.

▲ Custom-designed panels covering the upper door and lower freezer compartments of this state-of-the-art refrigerator blend the appliance into its Arts and Crafts surroundings. Reproduction hammered-copper handle pulls and hinges match those used throughout the kitchen cabinetry.

About Contractors

Hiring a contractor is the most important part of your research. Take your time to learn everything you can, and find someone who specializes in historic homes. Not only will this person be managing the project and your budget, but he or she also should be experienced enough so that unexpected situations—typical in older houses—don't waste more money or time than they need. Demolition can often be a revealing experience—you'll want someone on your team who can offer more than one solution.

Contractors are licensed and regulated by state agencies. To find an expert, start by getting a referral from someone you know. Nothing beats the word of a happy former customer. Otherwise, contact your local historical society for a list of qualified contractors in your area. Before starting, remember to sign a written agreement with your contractor that details the parameters of the project, materials to be used, a payment schedule, and start and finish dates.

▶ A large, open kitchen offers a mix of new and nostalgic with its frame-and-panel cabinetry, brushed-nickel bin-pull hardware, white subway tiles, farm sink, and stainless steel appliances. A traditional wood floor anchors the base cabinets, while a granite countertop provides a durable work surface.

▶ Raising the ceiling high above the upper cabinets in this Prairie home allows enough space for a plant ledge bathed in natural light from the skylight.

Mission Makeover

HOMEOWNERS DENISE AND KEITH MANOY decided to maximize the efficiency of space in their 1930s Mission-style Bungalow kitchen by working with the original layout. By moving the washer and dryer from a recessed area in the kitchen to an outside porch, the couple used the space to create an arched cooking alcove. They then removed the door to an enclosed pantry, creating easy access to the butler's pantry. A central work island connects the stove, refrigerator, and pantry areas while providing additional workspace. The original ironing-board bay serves as a knickknack shelf for family collectibles.

▲ The homeowners decided to use a combination of base cabinets and open shelving to store kitchen goods in the butler's pantry.

▲ The work island takes its design from paneled doors used throughout the house, while a new terra cotta floor underlines the Mission style.

◄ A standard 30-in. stove fits nicely between two work surfaces to provide a sheltered area for hot food items. Overhead, narrow open shelves keep herbs and spices within reach.

Bathrooms

Bathrooms have become a benchmark for comfort. Having an adequate number of them in a home is probably at the top of the list of every owner undertaking a renovation or building new. As with many older homes, this is a frequent issue in most vintage Arts and Crafts homes and Bungalows. And it's an issue that impacts resale value. But unlike earlier period-style homes, Arts and Crafts– and Bungalow-style homes were built with indoor plumbing, which makes the job of expanding or adding on a whole lot easier.

One of the most important things to consider when making over a bathroom—or any room—is to work within the derivative style of the home. A plain Prairie-inspired vanity, for example, would look out of place in a Mission-style Bungalow bath decorated in bold and brightly colored tile.

A good starting point is to examine the existing space. It may be that there is a simple solution. If functionality is a primary concern, then perhaps redesigning the space to accommodate a more practical layout and updating the fixtures with reproductions are all that are needed.

But if it's actual space that needs to be carved out of an adjacent room or closet, the project becomes more of an undertaking. For example, an extra bedroom might be converted into space for a new

▶ **This view from the vanity shows how careful planning can accommodate upscale bathroom conveniences. Here, a beadboard enclosure around the spa tub creates a private area for the toilet, while the vanity enclosure hides a walk-in steam shower.**

▲ Relatively unchanged since 1904, this Bungalow bathroom retains it original claw-foot tub, while the sink and toilet are replacements based on period styling. Casement windows reveal the bathroom's location under the eaves of the roofline where extra storage is utilized by a drop-down linen compartment.

▲ This original bathroom with its striking tilework shows how little basic bathroom configurations have changed over the years. The layout features a pedestal sink with porcelain handles across from the bathtub. The bumped-out wall of the tub enclosure provides the space for a walk-in shower, just opposite the toilet.

bath. This would save the cost and time commitment involved in building an addition but still entails construction.

Or look for hidden spaces. The room beneath a front staircase is often the perfect spot for a small powder room. Often, a first-floor closet can be used to hide plumbing for a new upstairs bathroom.

▼ ► Untouched since it was first built in 1930, this bathroom shows just how important colorful tiles and the arch motif are to the overall character of Mission-style Bungalows. The striking contrast of the light- and dark-blue border tile against the pale-yellow field tile recalls colorful Mediterranean pottery and hints at an emerging Art Deco style.

Finding Fixtures

Replacing a broken bathroom fixture can be a real feat. Finding matching styles is tough, but locating the exact color is often even harder. You may find yourself, like Denise Manoy and her daughter Brynne, scouring salvage yards and surfing eBay® for a purple-pink toilet, circa 1930.

(They eventually found their prize in a salvage yard in Fort Worth, Tex.)

Before you begin your search or place any on-line bids, be sure to take the measurements of the space where the replacement fixture is to go. These fixtures are often available in a variety of sizes, so don't assume there's a standard.

This new bathroom combines restrained, Mission-inspired tilework with Arts and Crafts styling as seen in the storage unit, which also doubles as a room divider. The unit's quartersawn oak and hammered hardware is replicated in the design of the medicine cabinet.

A Better Bathroom

HOMEOWNERS JENNY AND KEVIN MORAN decided to add on a much-needed master bathroom to their 1912 Prairie-style home. Jenny wanted a claw-foot tub, a double-basined vanity, and a separate water closet, while Kevin wanted a steam shower. Kevin, an architect, used his design skills to fit the many fixtures into their limited space. Kevin used the wall farthest from the door to hide the toilet, while the remaining wall accommodates the steam shower. To finish the room, window casings and partitioned glazed-panel designs were duplicated from the home's original designs.

Master Bath

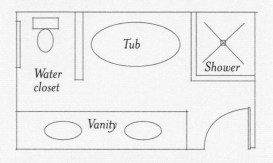

A new addition was built to accommodate a master suite that included a modest-sized bathroom. Two sinks, a steam shower, a private water closet, and a tub fit into an area just 7 ft. by 10 ft.

◀ **The reproduction claw-foot tub takes center stage in its own private alcove. It features a hand-held personal shower and a slate-covered shelf that's handy for bathing articles.**

◀ Re-creating the historic nature of an Arts and Crafts bathroom doesn't mean home-owners need do without. This bathroom incorporates many features of original designs such as the five-panel door and headboard paneling with new, state-of-the-art plumbing fixtures.

Make a List

Updating an older home to accommodate a kitchen or a bath or to gain additional closet space can be a tremendous time and financial commitment. Careful planning is important. It would be foolish to embark on a major project without considering your resources, but don't forget to dream. For starters, make a list. If you are updating a kitchen, for example, write down everything you've always wanted.

Next, imagine yourself living in it. Consider the layout. Is this a room you plan to eat in? Cook many meals in? Will it be a formal place or one where you might talk to guests or family while meals are being prepared? Think about how this room needs to fit in with the rest of the house and to what degree it should reflect the historical nature of the house. Once you've completed your wish list, you can begin to prioritize the items with an eye toward budget and time limitations.

▶ Bungalow homes introduced many space-saving features such as this corner sink, which has separate faucets for hot and cold water.

▶ A new bathroom mixes current trends with old ones. Glossy white subway tile and a period-inspired sink contrast nicely with the limestone floor and wainscot cap kept in an unpolished, matte finish. A newly designed medicine cabinet takes its cue from Prairie-style woodwork seen throughout the original parts of the house.

▶ An oak vanity with glass knobs draws from Arts and Crafts styling in this new bathroom, while reproduction wall sconces complete the theme.

▶ ▼ Mottled bright-blue subway tile and pink and black border tile strike a vivid contrast against the hexagonal floor tiles and purplish-pink plumbing fixtures in this original 1930 Mission-style Bungalow bathroom.

IN HISTORY

The earliest American patent for a toilet, or water closet as it was referred to at the time, was issued in 1875. Since then, many inventors have improved on the design and function, resulting in the flush toilet system. Today, many new bathrooms in period homes are designed with a separate space for the water closet. Perhaps this has something to do with the fact that the very first ones were located outdoors.

Bed, Bath, and Bungalow

When the owners of a 1917 Craftsman-style Bungalow needed a bigger master bedroom and bath, they hired Massachusetts architect Peter LaBau to come up with a plan. By taking in the space from two sleeping porches, a new master suite with additional closet space, a dressing area, and a new bathroom was created without changing the footprint of the original house.

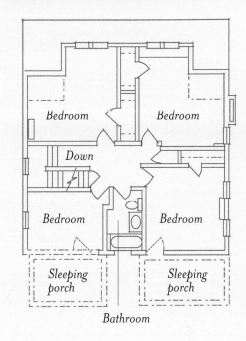

Second Floor, Before

By connecting what once were two upstairs sleeping porches, the homeowners now enjoy a master suite with a dressing area and master bath.

Second Floor, After

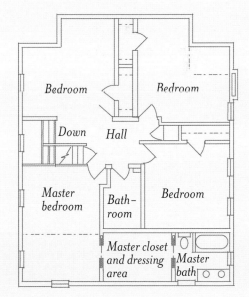

The new master bathroom features an Arts and Crafts–style vanity from Restoration Hardware, while the black and white hexagonal floor tile and subway tile wainscot capture an authentic interpretation of interior finishes common in turn-of-the-century Bungalow bathrooms.

Storage

There's a reason why these older homes have less storage space: It just wasn't needed. People who lived in original Bungalows didn't have as many clothes, gear, books, and machines. But we put a higher priority on space these days. And even though many Bungalows were meant to be modest, Bungalow owners today really need to think creatively when it comes to finding or adding on more space.

CLOSETS

Let's start with closets. One way to get the most out of these small areas is to maximize the vertical space inside. Specifically, removing the overhead shelf and hanging two rods, one above and one below, will double the room in the closet for hanging clothes. Using the prefabricated closet components from a local hardware store should not be considered taboo.

Planning for additional closets in older homes is one of the most difficult tasks. As with adding bathrooms, many fixes require taking over adjoining bedroom space to accommodate the plan or building on a new addition. Another solution is to build the new closet in the corner of the bedroom.

◄ Maximizing the space in a newly built walk-in closet, a bench surrounded by drawers keeps socks and stockings handy and provides a seat to use when putting them on.

Space Case

Compensating for the modest scale of Bungalow homes, builders at the turn of the 20th century often provided built-in storage to take advantage of otherwise unused space. If your Bungalow home lacks built-ins, consider adding your own. The space under a staircase can accommodate recessed drawers, cabinets, or cupboards, while a wall at the end of a hallway might yield enough space for narrow shelving.

◄ A new addition provides space for a generous master bedroom in this Prairie-style home from 1917. Built-out closets reminiscent of old wardrobes or armoires separate clothes into his and hers and are spaced far enough apart to create a private alcove for the bed. The closet's details mimic door and window patterns in the gridlike arrangement of the moldings.

Inside and Outside the Box

Bungalows are cherished for the added flexibility that their floor plans often present. This new Jamestown, R. I., Bungalow is no exception. For one, despite the cold climate, the homeowners make year-round use of a veranda that links the main house with an office over the garage. This rustic open space features massive windows that provide light and views, extending the sense of the outdoors within.

Inside, the home is at once traditional and practical. Exposed beams, pine flooring, and stained paneling all speak to Arts and Crafts styling. Sitting in the center of the first floor, the stone fireplace ties the kitchen, living room, and dining room together while delineating the bounds of each space.

Built-in furniture, like the home-office space constructed against the back wall of the fireplace, highlight the house's efficient planning. By working with local materials and the traditional Bungalow blueprint, these homeowners were able to create a modern classic.

▲ This storage wall makes clever use of space that might otherwise be overlooked.

◀ Bungalows often incorporated local resources, like this New England home, which features shingle siding.

◀ By installing windows instead of screens on this veranda, the owners converted a seasonal space to one that could be enjoyed in cold weather, too. Sofas and chairs are a welcoming addition, too.

▼ No crag or cranny is ignored as the space created by the staircase becomes an intimate nook with the addition of a loveseat.

▲ Although this built-in bureau is new, it's right at home in this Bungalow, where it contributes to an uncluttered look and offers space to keeps things organized.

▶ Storage space in this guest bedroom was easily created by bumping out the closet from the inside wall. Double doors minimize the space needed for door swings and were designed using the same molding and trim features seen on the original bedroom door.

▲ Locating the closet near the bedroom door gives uninterrupted wall space between it and the corner, while the pocket door keeps traffic flowing in and around the bedroom.

▶ **A built-in linen cabinet is original to this early Bungalow.**

Built-In Bonus

WHILE PLANNING FOR CLOSET SPACE
in the spare bedroom of their Mission-style
home, the owners got more than they had
expected. In this solution, two shallow
closets were built out from an exterior wall,
each one extending right up to the window
that sat in between. This presented a
perfect opportunity, so the owners had a
window seat installed in order to provide
additional storage and a handy place to sit.

The window seat between these closets
features a hinged lid.

WINDOW SEATS AND BOOKSHELVES

Today's homeowners have realized how practical old window seats
really are—from providing a cozy little space for curling up and
reading to offering out-of-the-way storage for those items only used
a few times a year. A hinged lid makes for easy access to the storage
area below. A window seat's design and detailing can be taken from
the ever-present inglenooks.

Bookshelves are the least intrusive type of storage solution,
whether they are built floor to ceiling, recessed in an existing wall, or
simply run against the wainscoting. Shelving that matches the
woodwork blends the most seamlessly.

▲ An unlikely space for shelving, the small
wall cavity just above plumbing pipes gives
easy access to soaps and shampoos while
showing off the homeowner's collection of
Arts and Crafts pottery.

Pure Prairie Home

OR JENNY AND KEVIN MORAN, finding enough space for a new master bedroom suite, gourmet kitchen, wine room, laundry room, breakfast nook, and powder bath within their 1912 Prairie-style home was impossible, so they decided to build an addition. Since Kevin's architectural practice has worked on numerous restoration projects on other historic homes in his Dallas neighborhood, he had many good ideas.

The couple decided to remove the old kitchen and sleeping porch, salvage what materials they could, and expand from there. The result is a remarkable

▲ The new rear addition matches the front down to the metal railings and Moorish finials on the upstairs balcony. The manu-facturer of the home's original 1912 tin roof was still in business, so the owners were able to find more of the same design and materials for their section of roof.

▶ The breakfast nook incor-porates molding details seen in the original dining room. A reproduction Stickley dining set and corner cabinet appro-priately feature Frank Lloyd Wright-designed dinnerware.

▲ An inside hallway connects the kitchen to the utility area, complete with wine rack, open pantry, powder bath, and laundry room. Doors and doorknobs were salvaged from the teardown, while trim and moldings duplicate the home's original designs.

1,000-sq.-ft. addition matched so closely to the original house that it's almost undetectable from the outside and full of Arts and Crafts styling on the inside.

The kitchen is equipped with high-end appliances balanced against rich oak cabinetry with beadboard insets. Characteristic Prairie-style muntins divide the glass into geometric patterns in the upper cabinets. The kitchen and adjoining breakfast room take in views of the back porch and garden.

▲ Instead of French doors opening out to the back porch, Jenny and Kevin Moran opted for windows so the flow of traffic between kitchen workspaces was not impeded.

Special Spaces

Families are spending more time together, sharing in meal preparation, watching movies, or getting the homework done. The layouts of original Arts and Crafts– and Bungalow-style houses are open but not necessarily spacious enough for these activities, so where do the people who live in these homes gather? Finding this special area may require remodeling the attic, for example, or part of the cellar. Or you might find yourself removing the wall of an upstairs bedroom and opening it up to the central hallway.

Other options include designing a new kitchen large enough to accommodate a family area, where the television and surround-sound system can be installed should they be on the wish list. Combined spaces like this can be designed with sensitivity to the historic nature of the house by borrowing Arts and Crafts details from other parts of the home. For example, any new cabinetry installed for housing the television and stereo equipment should be made of, say, quartersawn oak with hammered-copper hardware if this matches nearby cabinetry. Reproduction light fixtures can be used throughout to unify the new ones with the original interior.

▲ The rear entry in a Bungalow home functions as a mudroom. Here, the homeowners opted for almost school-like lockers for their three children, giving each their own space for coats, homework (in the drawers below), and shoes. Out of reach of little hands are winter coats, boots, and backyard toys.

◀ Craftsman styling was used in adding a work area that runs just beneath the windowsills in this period home.

Bungalows were designed with mudrooms off the back entrance to the house. Making the most of this space and resourcefully outfitting it for today's living might be as simple as adding a peg rail for hanging coats and umbrellas. Stackable cubes work well for sorting out and storing pet supplies or the kids' toys for outdoor play, and they maximize the vertical space.

◄ Only part of this room was taken over for a home office. Built-in cabinets, shelves, and cubbies keep things organized, while the detailing picks up woodwork patterns found elsewhere in the room.

A Multipurpose Kitchen

WITH THREE ACTIVE CHILDREN and a husband and wife who sometimes bring work home from the office, this Minneapolis family needed a space large enough for all to gather and work on specific tasks. The solution was a new kitchen designed to accommodate a cozy family gathering around the fireplace, a homework area, and a home office. This multipurpose kitchen features Arts and Crafts styling common to the couple's neighborhood yet remains utterly modern in its design and function.

▲ On the opposite side of the kitchen, a fireplace keeps the room cozy, while a wall with a chalkboard provides just the right privacy for a home office.

▼ Compact in its design and efficiently outfitted with file drawers and mail sorters, this built-in desk is specifically designed to complement the kitchen cabinetry.

◀ A central work island gives the kids plenty of room to spread out while the evening meal is prepared. The room is large enough so that carefully placed windows allow the outdoors in without sacrificing room for upper cabinets.

This room, situated along the upstairs central hallway, acts as a gathering space where the family reads, watches television, or plays games. Its compact design maximizes the space by providing ample shelving for toys, games, and books. A cozy window seat has handy lower drawers to store CDs and DVDs.

FIVE

Today's Classic Interior

IVING IN AN OLD HOUSE doesn't have to mean living in one that's uncomfortably cold, hot, or dark just to create an authentic interior. Although original Bungalows had the most modern of conveniences for their time, these innovations are outdated by today's standards. Even historic landmarks have climate control these days. Any owner of a classic house should not feel constrained by accuracy when adding or improving the amenities in it, especially when it comes to essentials such as heating, air-conditioning, and lighting. First and foremost, a house should be a home.

Heating a home at the turn of the 20th century was not a problem, and solutions varied by geographic region. In the South and Southwest, a fireplace or small gas-burning stove was adequate to take away the chill on a cold night. For homes in the Northeast and Midwest, either gas- or oil-fueled boilers were the standard. These boilers heated water that was distributed by pipes to radiators located throughout the house.

In today's newer homes, heating and air-conditioning are often handled by forced-air systems. These systems distribute warm or cool air through a network of ducts that run between the walls, ceilings, and floors. Forced-air systems are an option for updating old heating and cooling systems. A heating and air-conditioning specialist can determine the safety and efficiency of the boiler unit in a vintage Bungalow and make suggestions on updating or replacing the equipment based on the size and limitations of the home. Perhaps the biggest deciding

◄ The simply designed fireplace with brick surround and oak mantel in this Craftsman Bungalow complements the richness of the wainscoting behind it. The firebox opening is fitted with a cast-iron front, which radiates heat more efficiently. ► Although this plain style—the quintessential copper lamp with mica shade—was prevalent in early Craftsman Bungalows, highly ornate lighting fixtures with art-glass shades also were popular.

▲ Two fireplaces in a 1905 Craftsman-style Bungalow in Texas were the home's only sources of heat. The fire screen radiated warmth throughout the living and inglenook areas, while an additional fireplace heated two bedrooms.

▲ The original cast-iron fire screen has been restored to its copper-plated finish to highlight a rosette medallion tied up with ribbons. The ornamentation hints at a classical style echoed throughout the house.

factor is just how much homeowners can afford to spend to get what they want.

Bungalow fireplaces offered warmth and atmosphere to family life in a time before television and computer games and are enjoyed just as much today as they once were. Many people who uncover old renovation work may find a fireplace behind plaster or wallboard. This happy discovery should always be thoroughly inspected before being used. Loose bricks, mortar, or tile in the chimney, firebox, hearth, and surround can pose a safety hazard.

In addition to heating concerns, today's electrical needs usually far exceed the capacities of these older homes, as many homes still utilize old knob-and-tube wiring and fuse boxes. When Bungalows were first built, lighting was the primary reason to bring electricity into the home since gas was used to fire up the boiler and run the kitchen stove. Even the icebox was kept cold with just a block of ice.

Bungalow Bells

There are a few modern amenities that we don't even think about today, such as doorbells. With the noise of television sets and stereos, who could possibly hear a knock at the door? Now, it is possible to have a doorbell that's in keeping with the nature of Arts and Crafts design and will fit in with many interiors.

▲ This doorbell is made to look as if it were crafted by hand.

▲ Characteristic of Craftsman homes, this doorbell features a typical grid cutout pattern.

▲ Blending in with the Arts and Crafts interior, this doorbell mimics the vertical slats and hand-pegged joinery found in Stickley-styled furnishings.

In our time, we run far more electrical devices. Things we take for granted today, like air-conditioning, were not yet invented—the last Bungalows were built in the 1930s. Obviously, we need greater amperage today because more of the things in the home are powered by electricity. Having 100 amps is now considered standard for a typical home running kitchen appliances, multiple television sets, computers, and stereos. Back then, though, this power source was an exciting innovation. In fact, many light fixtures celebrated its appearance. Unfortunately, many lamps lacked shades of any kind, which contributed to poor lighting and resulted in uncomfortable glare problems.

By updating your home's heating system, adding an air-conditioning system, and investing in the complete rewiring of your house, your Bungalow will not only be more comfortable but also safer. This chapter offers solutions for integrating these modern conveniences into vintage-style homes without disrupting the historic flavor.

Fireplaces

When Frank Lloyd Wright designed a house, he designed everything from the floor plan to the furniture. Wright considered the fireplace to be the heart of the home, so he made it the anchor of the Prairie-style houses he designed. He often placed a cozy inglenook near the fireplace, using it as a focal point within the room.

No longer the primary heat source of homes, fireplaces in Bungalows—whether Craftsman, Mission, Prairie, or Arts and Crafts—were a featured design element in the living room. Framed by built-in bookshelves or window seats, the design of the fireplace fit the character of the architectural style.

These stylistic differences often determined the materials used for hearth and surround, such as the prevalence of tile in the Mission style and the use of brick hearths and surrounds with heavy wooden mantels for Craftsman and Prairie styles.

The style of a Bungalow tells us about the shape of the firebox opening and the configuration of the chimney. For example, it is not uncommon to find an arched opening in a Mission-style fireplace with a projecting chimney tapered toward the ceiling, while a Prairie-style Bungalow might have a simple square opening with the chimney flue concealed behind a wall of plaster. Regardless of shape, the commonality between the derivative Arts and Crafts styles is the consistent use of natural, organic materials such as brick, stone, tile, and wood.

▲ A close look at this fireplace shows how organic materials such as clay tile, wood, and brick come together to create a Craftsman-inspired mantel and surround. The overmantel is made with simple panels, framed by stiles and rails, and topped off with a plain cornice.

▶ Regardless of geographic location, a Bungalow living room is not complete without a fireplace. This example uses brick for both surround and hearth, while a wood mantel incorporates raised blocks typical of Craftsman detailing.

◀ Made from quartersawn oak and inspired by the designs of Arts and Crafts architect Charles Rennie Mackintosh, this fireplace mantel incorporates the prototypical four-block grid in its corners. The top of the mantel extends beyond its pilasters, which are tapered to emphasize mass and proportion.

Classic Update

A newly built Shingle home incorporates many design features of the English Arts and Crafts movement, namely the use of organic materials. The TV room features a large fireplace with fieldstone taken from the natural surroundings on Martha's Vineyard, Mass. Other materials such as quartersawn white oak used for the millwork of the mantel, crown molding, and built-ins complete the architectural features of the room.

The gentle arch of the fireplace opening subtly reinforces the curvature of the barrel-vaulted ceiling and alcove. Shaped brackets support the quartersawn white oak mantel.

◄ ▲ Original features of this 1924 Mission-style home include a Rookwood tile fireplace with an unusual wooden mantel held in place by two tile brackets. The mottled green and amber matte glaze of the tiles adds visual depth, while a characteristically oversized keystone marks the opening of the firebox.

▲ The dramatic architecture of this room is enhanced by the series of built-ins flanking a fireplace inspired by Mackintosh's designs. More modern in its appearance, the white fireplace, with its sweeping mantel and bold geometric designs, resembles Mackintosh furniture designs of the period.

◄ A corner fireplace in the bedroom of this 1905 kit home features an extraordinary cast-iron fire screen that helps radiate heat into a second bedroom through a connecting door. The red pine mantel with tapered brackets displays a subtle refinement.

Rookwood Pottery

Maria Longworth Nichols's idea of turning what was once women's craft into a profitable business began in 1880 with the founding of Rookwood Pottery in Cincinnati, Ohio. First known for its matte-glaze vases with botanical-inspired motifs, Rookwood Pottery created an architectural department that supplied tile to various building projects throughout America in 1902. Tile was embossed with flora and fauna designs with matte glazes in green, dark brown, orange, yellow, and pink.

The tile quickly became a feature of Bungalow-style homes, in particular Arts and Crafts Bungalows. It was used on walls as well as on fireplaces and hearths.

Both the fireplace and the copper andirons are original to this 1916 Arts and Crafts–style home. Small accent tiles depicting delicate flowers provide visual balance to the large keystone above its opening. The mantel is made entirely of Rookwood tile and is supported by three pressed tile brackets that feature potted tulips.

► The rounded arch of this fireplace opening is more common in Mission style Bungalows and often mimics cased door openings or recessed niches elsewhere in these houses. Photo © www.carolynbates.com, Sandra Vitzthum Architect, LLC.

▲ The simple arch of a brick fireplace is enhanced with a terra cotta plaque featuring a stylized bird and oak-leaf design. Photo © www.carolynbates.com, Sandra Vitzthum Architect, LLC.

► Although the fireplace in this 1926 California Mission-style Bungalow looks like rough-cut stonework, it is actually cast plaster.

Considered the heart and soul of homes, fireplaces were designed to be the focal point of Bungalow living rooms. Symmetrically placed built-ins, bookcases, or windows framed the centrally located fireplace, while decorative tile, wood, brick, or stone accentuated the surround and hearth.

Variations of the chimney design range from those seen only from the outside, which were made from stone or brick, to interior chimneys made from stucco or brick. Hooded chimneys are more common in the Spanish-influenced Mission homes.

◄ A Mission-style Bungalow prominently features an arched fireplace framed by two art-glass windows. The fire-resistant quality of stucco makes it the perfect material here, while the matte-glazed tile on the surround and hearth protect from soot. A small niche replaces the traditional mantel.

Mission Tradition

OWNERS KEITH AND DENISE MANOY decided to maximize the features of their nearly intact Mission-style Bungalow by emphasizing the living room's generous proportions and fine detailing. The original Rookwood tile on the fireplace inspired the color scheme for the room's interior furnishings, as well as Keith's painting seen hanging over the mantel.

Contrasting with the smoothness of the pottery tile, highly textured stucco walls are bathed in warm ochre paint. White paint highlights the crown moldings' intricate details. The moldings emphasize the coarse stucco wall surface.

A detailed and highly ornate mantel of Rookwood pottery tile features patterns replicated in the room's plaster crown moldings in this Mission home from 1930.

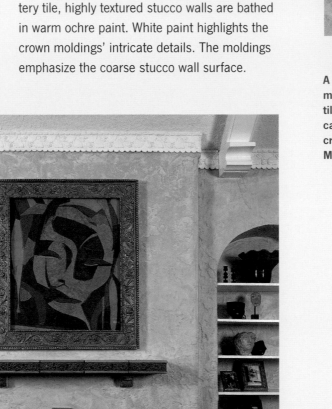

◄ Homeowners added space and scale to this Craftsman Bungalow living room when they removed a ceiling to reveal the rafters and rebuilt a wider, taller fireplace from the original River Rock design.

▼ A large hooded fireplace in the English Arts and Crafts tradition unifies the space between the living area and the gallery above in this new Arts and Crafts home. Photo © www.carolynbates.com, Sandra Vitzthum Architect, LLC.

► Iridescent tile decorates the central fireplace in the dining room of architects Greene and Greene's Gamble House in Pasadena, Calif.

► Corinthian columns decorating this 1920s Bungalow fireplace are indicative of the emerging Neo-Colonial style, with its emphasis on classical details.

A small fireplace tucked into the corner of this Craftsman-style room uses multi-colored matte-glaze tile to contrast with the dark, rich wood grain of the mantel.

IN HISTORY

Inspired by Japanese designs and the English Arts and Crafts movement, architects Charles Greene and Henry Greene integrated pure geometry with honest, organic materials in their California Bungalows. They built elaborate homes for a wealthy clientele. This and the fact that the brothers' designs appeared in numerous pattern books on Bungalows helped expand the influence of their work far beyond the California coast.

Classic Climate Control

For homes located in the colder areas of the country, the fireplace augmented the home's primary heating system: the boiler. Located in the cellar, boilers were at the heart of the system. A cast-iron radiator, sized according to the dimensions of the room, provided heat and was a most-efficient means of distributing the warmth. In today's homes, radiators are still effective heaters. It is often the boilers that need replacing for better energy efficiency.

HEATING, VENTILATING, AND AIR-CONDITIONING

Although air-conditioning was first introduced in the 1920s, it was not a common feature in modern homes until the mid-20th century. Now, because air-conditioning is a part of modern life, manufacturers of climate-control systems have made improvements in designing equipment that will keep your house cool while remaining unobtrusive.

Forced-air systems capable of delivering both heat and cool air can replace old radiators, although many homeowners may opt to use a combination of both since radiators add charm and character to a house. Concealed in vertically stacked closets, inconspicuously dropped ceilings, or run up from the basement through floor cavities, ductwork made from sheet metal or small, flexible plastic tubing can deliver the required amount of thermal comfort in a historic house.

High-velocity heating, ventilating, and air-conditioning (HVAC) systems are a more recent advance in climate control, yet the technology is new and costly. These air systems deliver hot or cold air through plastic flexible tubing as small as 3 in. in diameter. The size of the tubing allows it to be bent in and around tight areas behind walls and inside closets or to be run into the ceiling from attic space above.

▼ Hidden by decorated but unobtrusive covers, boiler-fed hot water or steam radiators were standard in Bungalow homes.

◄ The radiator in the entry hall of this 1917 Bungalow home has a custom-designed cover, giving it the appearance of a piece of furniture.

► This new radiator (from Burnham) combines radiant heat with convection heat to provide a warm, comfortable environment in this kitchen remodel.

Early Bungalows were designed with numerous "low-tech" features for achieving a level of human comfort. Instead of air-conditioning, these Bungalows utilized attic fans to circulate air between rooms and casement windows for directing breezes. Even the large, overhanging eaves of the gable roof shielded the rooms from the heat of the midday sun, while screened-in sleeping porches brought in late-night breezes.

▲ Like the old gas stoves used to keep earlier Bungalows warm, the source of heat from a forced-hot-air system is located near the source of cold air—the window. The hot air rises, thus heating the room, while colder air falls and is warmed by the heater.

▲ All spaces in this 1910 Texas Bungalow connect through a series of operable doors or cased openings, thus allowing the attic fan to circulate fresh air from attic intakes to all parts of the home's interior. The attic fan works so well today that the homeowners don't feel the need for air-conditioning.

▲ This 1930s Mission-style Bungalow has a new HVAC system with ductwork running through the dropped ceiling of the central hallway.

▶ This new addition in a Midwestern Prairie Bungalow incorporates a modern heating and air-conditioning system. Air is delivered through vents concealed underneath the window seat and behind a custom-designed radiator cover.

▲ Discreetly hidden in the base of this window seat, new ductwork from the heating and air-conditioning system is covered by wooden grills.

The Perfect Temperature

Regardless of what type of heating, ventilation, and air-conditioning systems are in your home now—whether heatolator, gas stove, boiler, or attic fan—updating them will probably take some research. Regional differences dictate certain solutions. For example, do you rely on electricity, oil, or gas for your primary heating source? And how many days of the year will you need some sort of climate control? In the Southern regions, forced air is most practical, providing both heating and cooling delivered through a network of supply and return vents. Operating on electricity, these systems deliver airflow determined by thermostats.

Northern and Midwestern regions, where oil and gas lines feed into the older neighborhoods, benefit from boiler units, which circulate hot water or steam via well-placed radiators throughout the house. Updating the boiler and relying on an original attic fan may provide adequate cooling. Regardless of location, addressing these upgrades will certainly involve budgetary concerns. Consulting with a heating and air-conditioning specialist before starting any restoration or renovation work will give you an idea of the expense and scope of work involved.

◄ New and old systems such as a high-velocity air-conditioning system and a still-functioning forced-hot-water radiator make this 1915 Craftsman-style Bungalow a modern comfort.

▲ A high-velocity air-conditioning system with its small opening is barely detectable in the corner of this living room ceiling.

Lighting

Bungalows were one of the first housing types in America to feature electric lighting. The Victorian homes that came before them relied on gaslights. The design of lighting fixtures varied from a simple, exposed bulb hanging by its electrical wire to ceiling-mounted porcelain fixtures with embossed floral patterns painted in soft colors and bulbs without shades. Later, glass shades were designed to cover the bulb, which eliminated glare and helped create a softer, more diffuse light in the room.

The most common misconception people have about Bungalow lighting is that every light fixture in the home must look as though Frank Lloyd Wright designed it. This is often reinforced by manufacturers of Arts and Crafts lighting because that style is mostly what they sell. The easiest styles to find are angular and geometrically designed lighting featuring amber glass held in place by muntins arranged in a grid pattern.

What most owners of Bungalow houses don't realize is that there were many lighting options to choose from in the early 20th century, including the highly decorative styles produced by Tiffany Studios and Quezal, which featured delicate designs based on natural floral designs.

▲ **A 1916 Prairie-style home features an original light fixture complete with delicately shaped lotus-bud art-glass shades. Many mistakenly believe that light fixtures should follow strict geometric designs as used by Frank Lloyd Wright.**

▶ **This reproduction shower fixture with a metal medallion plate and art-glass shades recalls original designs produced by the Tiffany Studios in New York during the late 19th and early 20th centuries. Shower-type lights were used through out the house, from living and dining areas to bedrooms.**

◄ Push-button light switches were a standard feature of knob-and-tube wiring found in homes built before 1930.

▼ The living room in this 1908 Craftsman-style Bungalow incorporates both original and reproduction light fixtures. The central ceiling light made from bronze and stained glass is from the early 1900s, while the lanterns hanging from boxed beams are reproductions.

▲ One of the rarer styles of Bungalow lighting, this shower fixture seen hanging above the dining-room table is an original piece. Chandeliers like this were common in Craftsman-style Bungalows, yet their fragility and the value of the highly sought-after art-glass shades have caused many to disappear either through breakage or theft.

▲ The dining room in the Gamble House in Pasadena, Calif., shows how carefully light was integrated into the earliest of Arts and Crafts interiors. Made from wood and glass, the fixture is visually anchored to wooden details on the ceiling.

Uncovering the Right Light

If your vintage home has been stripped of its light fixtures, deciding what to replace them with may be challenging. How do you know with any certainty what was there originally? On one hand, it's not absolutely necessary to replace exactly what was there when the house was built. On the other hand, don't go too far afield. There are many modern styles to choose from, so select fixtures that are most appropriate to the home's architecture. Do some investigating; there may be bathroom fixtures or hallway fixtures still in place that hint at whether the original ones were either fancy or plain. Search the attic and basement for lighting remnants that may have never been thrown out. Also, since one builder often built comparable Bungalows within the same neighborhood, you might check with your neighbors for clues.

◄ Each lantern features art-glass shades held in place by thin muntins to create a nice counterpoint to the ceiling details in this Craftsman-style room.

▼ The most basic form of lighting in some of the earliest Bungalow designs features a bulb hanging by its electrical wire. These simply designed light fixtures recall nostalgia for earlier times without sacrificing style.

TYING IN TO THE ARCHITECTURE

The most important consideration when replacing the light fixtures in your Bungalow home is to make a selection that ties in to the inherent design of the architecture. For example, an angular Wright-inspired fixture would be out of place in a home built in the 1920s with Neo-Colonial influences. In addition, a Prairie-style home would look out of character if more elegant fixtures with Tiffany glass shades were used.

The work of New Yorker Louis Comfort Tiffany (1848–1933) is often confused with that of his jewelry designer father, Charles Lewis Tiffany. In 1885, Louis Comfort Tiffany patented his method of making opalescent glass, later to be called Favrile glass. Influenced by the Art Nouveau movement of the late 19th century, his glass designs featured highly stylized flowers, dragonflies, and other motifs inspired by nature. Decorative accessories for the home were sold through Tiffany Studios and included lamps, vases, and stained-glass windows. The company also produced rugs and textiles.

◄ ▲ Light fixtures within Arts and Crafts–style homes did not necessarily follow the strict gridlike geometry of the Wright-inspired Prairie styles. These fixtures feature soft, curvaceous lines with flower-bud glass shades evoking the influence of Tiffany Studios.

STYLE
your
WAY

Made in Mexico

WHEN HOMEOWNERS DENISE AND KEITH MANOY purchased their 1930s Mission-style Bungalow, the original light fixtures had been removed, including the ones on the outside porch. With only a wrought-iron and glass address plaque as well as examples seen on Mission homes in other nearby historic neighborhoods to go by, the couple plowed through stacks of lighting catalogs, hoping to find porch fixtures to match. It was by chance that they stumbled upon a store selling light fixtures from Mexico, where they found this perfect solution shown at right.

◀ Don't be surprised to find light fixtures like these in your Bungalow home. These original fixtures adorn the hallways of a 1924 Mission-style home that also incorporates many features of the emerging Neo-Colonial style that was gaining popularity during the late 1920s.

A Well-Lighted Place

When the owners of this Washington, D.C., Bungalow planned the renovation of their new residence, they were determined to create a home that maintained its pedigree and at the same time was convenient to live in. For them, this meant opening up the first floor, primarily so that from other rooms they could view the massive stone fireplace on the first floor that had inspired them to buy the house. Also, they wanted to restore the house's original detailing and modernize the bathrooms, kitchen, and closets.

Making the place functional meant having adequate light. They quickly determined that by using a mix of modern and period lighting fixtures, they could achieve their goal. Since many of the fixtures they liked were available new—quality reproductions are in abundance these days—they chose them over refurbishing antique fixtures. The result is a home that's remade with all its rich detail work. Of course, all the owners' hard work is beautifully illuminated in the Arts and Crafts style.

▲ The homeowners of this 1916 Washington, D.C., Bungalow replaced load-bearing walls with columns to open up the interior.

Mica-shaded sconces and a copper period-inspired chandelier in the Craftsman style combine with honest, exposed woodwork to complete the Arts and Crafts aesthetic of this home library.

Modern recessed-can fixtures work well with shiny work surfaces and natural light from the windows to brighten up the dark wood trim of this renovated kitchen.

A heavy brass ceiling fixture flanked by matching globes in the entranceway sets the formal tone for the rest of the house.

▼ Today's popularity of these nickel-plated wall sconces with frosted white shades actually had roots in Bungalow-designed bathrooms of the 1920s.

▲ Taking design cues from Wright, this new wall sconce recalls Prairie styling with its numerous grids that frame the light shade.

▲ The lanternlike shape of this wall sconce mimics the design of the outside porch light. The amber-colored art-glass shade uses bronze framing members to create the grid design more popular with Prairie-style houses.

◄ Lamps like these speak to the geometry of Mission-style furniture.

▲ No porch would be complete without a light designed in the architectural style of the house. This reproduction is appropriate for most Prairie- and Craftsman-style Bungalows, with its grid-patterned metal frame and frosted-glass shade.

◄ Reproduction wall sconces with frosted-glass shades accent the nostalgic look of this updated bathroom.

Old Is New Again

There are several options for replacing light fixtures in your Bungalow, ranging from searching through antique lighting stores, salvage yards, and eBay to purchasing new reproduction fixtures in styles inspired by antiques. For new additions, such as kitchens or family rooms where the historic nature of the house may only be hinted at, new fixtures loosely based on old designs might actually be more appropriate than old ones.

▶ The owners of this 1916 Arts and Crafts–style home are fortunate to have four of the home's original light fixtures like this one in the master bedroom. Extremely rare (most homes in this Dallas neighborhood had been stripped by vandals), this light fixture features its original Quezal art-glass shades.

◀ This new, three-arm fixture in brushed nickel was inspired by period fixtures from the 1920s with its frosted-glass shades and simple styling.

▲ New reproduction fixtures such as this one from Rejuvenation remain true to the original design with its cascading shower fixture and art-glass shades.

Resources

Carney Architects
215 S. King St.
Jackson, WY 83001
Phone: (307) 733-4000
Fax: (307) 733-1147
Web: www.carneyarchitects.com

David Whitney, Michael Grant,
Charles Rose
Charles Rose Architects Inc.
115 Willow Ave.
Somerville, MA 02144
Phone: (617) 628-5033
Fax: (617) 628-7033
Web: www.charlesrosearchitects.com

Peter LaBau
The Classic Group, Inc.
420 Bedford St.
Lexington, MA 02420
Phone: (781) 761-1200
Fax: (781) 761-1299
E-mail: cgi@theclassicgroup.net
Web: www.theclassicgroup.net

Dahlin Harris Homes, LLC
4061 N. Main St., Suite 200
Racine, WI 53402
Phone: (262) 639-2140
Fax: (262) 752-1895
Web: www.dahlinharris.com

Daron Tapscott, Architect
5230 Goodwin Ave.
Dallas, TX 75206
Phone: (214) 821-1755
Fax: (214) 826-4840
Web: daron@victorywebdesigns.com

Donna Guerra, ASID
DG&A Interior Design
5401 N. Central Expressway, Suite 305
Dallas, TX 75205
Phone: (214) 522-6716

Haynes-Roberts, Inc.
601 W. 26 St.
New York, NY 10001
Phone: (212) 989-1901

Lillian Heard
158 Berkely Rd.
Brooklyn, NY 11217

Bruce Holt
Corinth Building Service
304 Bryan Pl.
Cedar Hill, TX 75104
Phone: (214) 213-7757

Martha's Vineyard Construction Co., Inc.
Box 2169
Vineyard Haven, MA 02568

Moran & Murphy Architects, Inc.
4501 Swiss Ave.
Dallas, TX 75204
Phone: (214) 841-4507

Robert Orr & Associates
441 Chapel St. 2nd Fl.
New Haven, CT 06511
Phone: (203) 777-3387

Joseph G. Metzler & Steven Buetow
SALA Architects, Inc.
43 Main St. SE, Suite 410
Minneapolis, MN 55414

Salerno/Livingston Architects
363 5th Ave., 3rd Fl.
San Diego, CA 92101
Phone: (619) 234-7471
Fax: (619) 234-4625
Web: www.slarchitects.com

Sandy Vizthum, Architect
46 E. State St.
Montpelier, VT 05602
Phone: (802) 223-1806
E-mail: vitzthum@plainfield.bypass.com

South Mountain Co., Inc.
Red Arrow Rd.
West Tisbury, MA 02575
Web: www.somoco.com

Vujovich Design Build
275 Market St., Suite 141
Minneapolis, MN 53405
Web: www.vujovich.com

William Rennie Boyd, Architect
200 7th Ave., #110
Santa Cruz, CA 95062
Phone: (831) 465-9910
Fax: (831) 476-2025

SUPPLIERS

Architectural Products by
Outwater, L.L.C.
4 Passaic St.
P. O. Drawer 403
Wood-Ridge, NJ 07075
Phone: (800) 631-8375
Fax: (800) 888-3315
Web: www.archpro.com

Bradbury & Bradbury
P. O. Box 155
Benicia, CA 94510
Phone: (707) 746-1900
Fax: (707) 745-9417
Web: www.bradbury.com

Charles Rupert Designs Limited
2005 Oak Bay Ave.
Victoria, B.C. V8R 1E5
Canada
Phone: (250) 592-4916
Fax: (250) 592-4999
Web: www.charles-rupert.com

The Craftsman Homes Collection
PMB 343
2525 E. 29, Suite 10B
Spokane, WA 99223
Phone: (509) 535-5098
Web: www.crafthome.com

Crown Point Cabinetry
153 Charlestown Rd.
Claremont, NH 03743
Phone: (800) 999-4994
Fax: (800) 370-1218
Web: www.crown-point.com

Hammerworks
118 Main St.
Meredith, NH 03253
Phone: (603) 279-7352
6 Fremont St.
Worcester, MA 01603
Phone: (508) 755-3434
Web: www.hammerworks.com

J. R. Burrows & Company
P.O. Box 522
Rockland, MA 02370
Phone: (781) 982-1812
Fax: (781) 982-1636
E-mail: merchant@burrows.com
Web: www.burrows.com

Rejuvenation
2550 NW Nicolai St.
Portland, OR 97210
Phone: (888) 401-1900
Fax: (800) 526-7329
Web: www.rejuvenation.com

Sherwin-Williams
Web: www.sherwin-williams.com
for store locations

Wood-Mode Fine Custom Cabinetry
Web: www.wood-mode.com
for showroom locator

Index

Photo Credits